TIMELESS WISDOM

Lessons on Success and Fulfillment from History's Most Influential Minds

FELIX GRAYSON

MINDSPARK
PUBLISHING

*To those who seek meaning beyond measure,
and to the timeless wisdom that guides us all—
this book is for you.*

"What lies behind us and what lies before us are tiny matters compared to what lies within us."

— *Ralph Waldo Emerson*

ABOUT STONED PHILOSOPHER

Welcome to the *Stoned Philosopher* series—where timeless wisdom meets the modern world.

Each book distills powerful lessons from history's greatest minds, leaders, and thinkers—transforming their ideas into practical insights for today's challenges.

From mastering habits, calm, and resilience to understanding success, leadership, and meaning, this collection invites you to think deeper, live wiser, and see life from new perspectives.

Whether you're exploring *Modern Zen*, uncovering *The Wisdom of Warriors,* or seeking clarity through *The Art of Perspective*, every title offers a journey toward self-mastery and understanding.

Discover the full *Stoned Philosopher* collection and more at **FelixGrayson.com**, home of **Mind-Spark Publishing**—where knowledge, philosophy, and storytelling come together to spark lifelong curiosity.

FelixGrayson.com

Wisdom isn't something we find—it's something we grow into.

Let the journey begin.

CONTENTS

INTRODUCTION: THE JOURNEY TO TIMELESS FULFILLMENT

What does it mean to lead a successful life? Is it the accumulation of wealth, status, and achievements? Or does success lie in something deeper—something less tangible yet profoundly enduring? For centuries, humanity has wrestled with these questions, seeking answers not just in philosophy and literature but in the stories of those who have walked before us. The lives of history's most influential minds reveal a striking truth: true success and fulfillment are not confined to external markers but are found in the alignment of our actions with our values, the resilience we cultivate in adversity, and the connections we build with others.

This book is an invitation to embark on a journey—a journey guided by timeless wisdom, where the destinations are clarity, purpose, and meaning. It is not a road map to conventional success but a compass to navigate the paradoxes of modern life. In these pages, you will encounter the lessons of visionaries, leaders, and thinkers who dared to redefine what it means to live a life of significance. Their stories are not merely historical accounts but mirrors reflecting truths that are as relevant today as they were in their time.

A Search for Meaning in an Overwhelming World

We live in an age of paradox. On the one hand, the modern world offers unprecedented opportunities for success. Technological advancements have connected us across continents, and the barriers to achievement seem lower than ever before. Yet, paradoxically, this abundance often leaves us feeling overwhelmed, unfulfilled, and disconnected from what truly matters. The pressure to measure our worth by external standards—social media followers, financial milestones, or professional accolades—has never been greater. Amid this noise, the search for meaning becomes both urgent and elusive.

This book was born from the recognition that

fulfillment requires a different approach. It calls us to look beyond the surface and explore the deeper currents that shape our lives. Fulfillment is not a formula to be followed but a process of discovery, grounded in the timeless wisdom of those who have grappled with life's greatest questions.

The Timeless Lessons of Great Minds

The stories of history's most remarkable figures offer a wealth of insights for this journey. Marcus Aurelius, the Stoic emperor, found peace amid the chaos of ruling an empire by focusing on what lay within his control. Viktor Frankl, a survivor of unimaginable suffering, uncovered the transformative power of purpose in even the darkest circumstances. Helen Keller, undeterred by profound physical limitations, demonstrated that resilience and gratitude can illuminate paths to joy and connection. These figures and countless others remind us that fulfillment is not the absence of hardship but the ability to find meaning and growth within it.

Yet, this book is not simply a tribute to the past. It is a bridge between the lessons of history and the challenges of today. It connects ancient philosophies with modern psychology, blending timeless ideas with practical applications. The goal is not to prescribe a single path but to inspire you to forge your own, equipped with the tools and insights to navigate life's complexities.

A Guide to a Life Well-Lived

This book is structured to guide you through the core pillars of a meaningful and fulfilling life:

- **Inner Strength:** How can we cultivate resilience and self-discipline to weather life's storms? What practices can help us build the inner fortitude needed to persevere and grow?

- **Vision:** What does it mean to see beyond the immediate and imagine a future that aligns with our values? How can we challenge conventional thinking and embrace creativity and purpose?

- **Balance:** How can we harmonize ambition with contentment, action with reflection, and striving with being? What role does mindfulness play in achieving this balance?

- **Relationships:** How can we build meaningful connections that enrich our lives and the lives of others? What role do trust, empathy, and collaboration play in creating lasting bonds?

- **Legacy:** What kind of impact do we want to leave behind? How can we align our daily actions with a greater purpose that transcends our own lives?

- **Fulfillment:** How can we redefine success on our own terms, embracing gratitude, purpose, and growth as lifelong practices?

Each chapter delves into these themes, blending historical narratives, philosophical reflections, and actionable insights. Whether you are seeking clarity in a time of transition, resilience in the face of challenges, or inspiration to live more intentionally, this book offers a roadmap to help you navigate your journey.

An Invitation to Reflect and Act

As you embark on this journey, I encourage you to approach these pages with an open mind and a reflective heart. The insights you encounter here are not rigid prescriptions but sparks to ignite your own exploration. Take time to consider how the lessons resonate with your life, your values, and your aspirations. What does fulfillment mean to you? How can you align your daily choices with your vision for a meaningful life? These questions, more than any external measure, will guide you toward the answers you seek.

The process of reflection is only the beginning. Fulfillment is ultimately found in action—in the small, deliberate steps we take each day to create a life that aligns with our values and aspirations. Whether it is expressing gratitude, pursuing a passion, or nurturing a relationship, each action contributes to a larger narrative of meaning and purpose. This book is not an end but a beginning—a call to live with intention, courage, and curiosity.

A Journey Without End

Fulfillment is not a static achievement but a dynamic process that evolves with each stage of life. It is the resilience to adapt to change, the courage to pursue growth, and the wisdom to appreciate the present moment. As you move through the chapters of this book, you will find that fulfillment is less about reaching a final destination and more about the journey itself—a journey of becoming, creating, and connecting.

In the words of Ralph Waldo Emerson, "What lies behind us and what lies before us are tiny matters compared to what lies within us." This timeless wisdom reminds us that the seeds of fulfillment are already within us, waiting to be nurtured and brought to life. By engaging with the lessons of this book, you take the first step in cultivating a life that is not only successful but deeply meaningful.

The journey awaits. Let's begin.

CHAPTER 1: THE FOUNDATION OF SUCCESS – BUILDING INNER STRENGTH

Understanding the Core of Inner Strength

Inner strength is the unseen architecture of success, a silent force shaping decisions, endurance, and the ability to persevere. History offers countless examples of individuals whose inner fortitude enabled them to transcend their circumstances and achieve remarkable feats. Among the most celebrated of these figures is Marcus Aurelius, a Roman emperor and philosopher who epitomized stoic resilience. His reflections in *Meditations* provide a timeless roadmap to understanding and cultivating inner strength, blending philosophical inquiry with practical wisdom.

Marcus Aurelius lived during turbulent times, facing wars, plagues, and personal tragedies. Despite these challenges, he maintained his composure and governed with integrity. His secret lay in his ability to detach from external chaos and focus on his inner world, a principle central to stoic philosophy. For Marcus, inner strength was not merely the capacity to endure hardship but the ability to find clarity and purpose amidst life's trials. "You have power over your mind—not outside events. Realize this, and you will find strength," he wrote. This insight underscores the stoic belief that true power lies within, unaffected by external circumstances.

The core of inner strength begins with self-discipline. Discipline is often misunderstood as an external constraint, a set of rigid rules imposed upon oneself. However, stoics like Marcus Aurelius viewed it as a pathway to freedom. Discipline enables individuals to master their impulses and align their actions with their values. It creates a sturdy foundation for personal growth, allowing one to face challenges with equanimity and focus. Without discipline, emotions and desires can run unchecked, leading to chaos and regret. But with it, individuals gain control over their choices, forging a path toward purpose and fulfillment.

Mental resilience, another pillar of inner strength, is the capacity to adapt and thrive in the face of adversity. It is not a trait one is born with but a skill cultivated over time through experience and reflection. Marcus Aurelius's writings reveal his struggles with doubt, fear, and frustration, yet he repeatedly chose to return to the principles of stoicism to guide him. He treated every setback as an opportunity to practice resilience, asking himself not, "Why is this happening to me?" but rather, "How can I rise above this?" This mindset transforms obstacles into stepping stones, a principle echoed in modern psychology's concept of post-traumatic growth.

In today's world, where external pressures often feel relentless, Marcus's wisdom remains profoundly relevant. Consider the rise of mindfulness practices, which echo stoic teachings on the importance of inner awareness. Mindfulness encourages individuals to observe their thoughts and emotions without judgment, fostering a sense of detachment similar to the stoic principle of *apatheia*—freedom from irrational passions. By cultivating this practice, individuals can build resilience and clarity, anchoring themselves amidst the storms of modern life.

Practical applications of stoic principles can begin with small, deliberate actions. For instance, embracing discomfort, whether through physical challenges like exercise or mental ones like confronting fears, helps strengthen the will.

Marcus Aurelius often reminded himself to anticipate difficulties each day, viewing them as natural and inevitable. This practice, known as negative visualization, prepares the mind to face challenges without surprise or despair. By imagining potential obstacles, individuals can develop the mental preparedness to meet them with poise and resolve.

Another valuable exercise is the nightly reflection, a habit Marcus Aurelius likely practiced in writing *Meditations*. Taking time each evening to review one's actions, thoughts, and emotions fosters self-awareness and accountability. It allows individuals to identify areas for improvement while acknowledging progress, reinforcing the habits that contribute to inner strength. This practice aligns with modern strategies for personal growth, such as journaling and cognitive-behavioral techniques.

Ultimately, the foundation of inner strength lies in understanding one's purpose. For Marcus Aurelius, this meant living in harmony with nature and fulfilling his duty as a leader and a human being. He believed that aligning one's actions with a higher purpose provided the motivation and resilience needed to persevere. This concept resonates across cultures and philosophies, from the Japanese *ikigai*—a sense of purpose that makes life worth living—to the psychological theories of self-determination and intrinsic motivation.

Inner strength is not a destination but a continuous process of growth and refinement. It demands vigilance, effort, and a willingness to confront one's limitations. Yet, the rewards are profound: a life lived with intention, clarity, and an unshakeable sense of self. Marcus Aurelius's teachings remind us that the power to cultivate this strength resides within each of us, waiting to be discovered and nurtured.

As readers delve further into this chapter, they will encounter practical strategies and insights to deepen their understanding of self-control, habits, and the enduring role of inner strength in achieving success. By exploring these principles, they will uncover the timeless wisdom needed to navigate life's challenges with grace and determination. Inner strength, as Marcus Aurelius so eloquently taught, is not just the foundation of success—it is the essence of a life well-lived.

Mastering Self-Control in the Face of Adversity

Self-control is often portrayed as a simple act of willpower, a momentary decision to resist temptation or remain composed under pressure. Yet, as history and philosophy reveal, it is far more profound—a dynamic process of aligning one's thoughts, emotions, and actions with a higher purpose, even in the midst of life's greatest challenges. To master self-control is to embrace adversity not as an enemy, but as a teacher. This principle finds its embodiment in the lives of figures like Mahatma Gandhi, whose unwavering discipline turned personal hardships into a force for collective transformation.

Gandhi's philosophy of *satyagraha*, or "truth-force," was deeply rooted in self-control. He viewed it as an essential component of nonviolent resistance, a means to confront oppression without succumbing to anger or hatred. His ability to maintain composure under immense pressure—whether facing imprisonment, hunger strikes, or public criticism—stemmed from his conviction that true strength lay in mastering oneself. "The best way to find yourself is to lose yourself in the service of others," Gandhi wrote, linking self-control to the greater good. By reframing personal struggles as opportunities to serve a higher cause, he exemplified the transformative power of disciplined thought and action.

Philosophers and psychologists alike have emphasized the importance of reframing adversity as an opportunity for growth. Viktor Frankl, a Holocaust survivor and renowned psychiatrist, argued in *Man's Search for Meaning* that even in the most horrific circumstances, individuals retain the ability to choose their response. He described how fellow concentration camp inmates who maintained their dignity and humanity often did so by exercising self-control over their thoughts and attitudes. Frankl's insights reveal that the essence of self-control lies not in avoiding hardship but in finding meaning within it.

Modern research in psychology supports this view, highlighting the role of self-control in fostering resilience. The concept of emotional regulation, for example, emphasizes the ability to manage one's emotional responses to stressors. Studies have shown that individuals with strong emotional regulation skills are better equipped to navigate difficult situations, as they are less likely to be overwhelmed by fear or frustration. This aligns with historical examples like that of Theodore Roosevelt, who overcame childhood illness and personal tragedy by channeling his energy into purposeful pursuits. Roosevelt's life demonstrates that self-control is not just a reactive skill but a proactive strategy for shaping one's destiny.

Practical exercises can help cultivate this vital skill, beginning with the practice of mindfulness. By cultivating an awareness of one's thoughts and emotions without judgment, individuals can create a mental space between stimulus and response. This space, as described by Frankl, is where freedom lies—the freedom to choose a deliberate and constructive reaction. Mindfulness practices, such as deep breathing or meditation, have been shown to reduce stress and enhance self-control by fostering this sense of intentionality.

Another powerful tool is the art of reframing.

Adversity often feels overwhelming because it is perceived as a threat rather than a challenge. However, by consciously shifting one's perspective, it becomes possible to view setbacks as opportunities for growth. This principle is vividly illustrated in the life of Helen Keller, who overcame the dual challenges of blindness and deafness to become a renowned author and activist. Keller's triumph was not merely a testament to her perseverance but also to her ability to reframe her limitations as sources of strength. "Although the world is full of suffering, it is also full of the overcoming of it," she wrote, capturing the essence of turning adversity into opportunity.

In addition to mindfulness and reframing, setting clear and meaningful goals can enhance self-control by providing a sense of direction and purpose. When faced with adversity, individuals often falter due to a lack of clarity about their priorities. However, by defining what truly matters—whether it is personal integrity, family, or a professional aspiration—it becomes easier to stay focused and resist distractions. The life of Nelson Mandela offers a striking example of this principle. During his 27 years of imprisonment, Mandela maintained his sense of purpose by focusing on the vision of a free and equal South Africa. His ability to endure isolation and hardship without bitterness stemmed from his unwavering commitment to this goal, illustrating the profound connection between purpose and self-control.

Adversity, though often unwelcome, can serve as a crucible for character, forging qualities like patience, empathy, and resilience. This transformative potential is reflected in the Japanese concept of *kintsugi,* the art of repairing broken pottery with gold. Rather than disguising flaws, *kintsugi* celebrates them, turning fractures into features of beauty and strength. Similarly, mastering self-control allows individuals to integrate their struggles into a narrative of growth, creating a life that is not diminished by adversity but enriched by it.

Self-control also requires self-compassion. While the term might suggest an uncompromising discipline, true self-control acknowledges human imperfection and embraces the process of learning from failure. This perspective is exemplified by Abraham Lincoln, who faced repeated political defeats before becoming one of America's most revered leaders. Lincoln's ability to persevere through setbacks was grounded in his capacity for self-reflection and forgiveness, both of himself and others. His story underscores that self-control is not about suppressing emotions but about channeling them constructively, transforming disappointment into determination.

As readers delve into this chapter, they are encouraged to reflect on their own relationship with adversity. What challenges have tested their self-control, and how might they reframe these experiences as opportunities for growth? By examining the lives of historical figures and embracing practices like mindfulness, reframing, and goal-setting, individuals can begin to master self-control in the face of life's inevitable trials. This mastery, as history reveals, is not only the key to overcoming hardship but also the foundation of a fulfilled and purposeful life.

In the words of Marcus Aurelius, "You have power over your mind—not outside events. Realize this, and you will find strength." These timeless words remind us that while we cannot control the storms of life, we can control how we navigate them, emerging not unscathed but stronger, wiser, and more resilient.

The Role of Habits in Building Strength

Habits are the invisible threads that weave the fabric of our lives. They dictate our routines, shape our decisions, and ultimately define who we become. For those seeking to cultivate inner strength, habits serve as the scaffolding on which resilience, discipline, and character are built. While grand gestures and monumental efforts may capture attention, it is often the quiet, consistent actions—repeated day after day—that lay the foundation for enduring success.

Aristotle once said, "We are what we repeatedly do. Excellence, then, is not an act but a habit." This profound observation highlights the transformative power of habits, suggesting that greatness arises not from isolated acts but from patterns ingrained into daily life. The ancient Greek philosophers recognized that habits have a cumulative effect, shaping one's character and destiny over time. This principle remains as relevant today as it was in Aristotle's time, offering a framework for understanding how habits can fortify inner strength.

Historical figures provide compelling examples of how habits serve as cornerstones of personal fortitude. Benjamin Franklin, one of America's founding fathers, was a master of self-improvement through habitual practice. Franklin famously devised a system of thirteen virtues, such as temperance, frugality, and humility, which he sought to cultivate in himself. Each week, he focused on a specific virtue, reflecting on his progress daily. While he admitted he never attained perfection, Franklin credited this methodical approach to habit formation with much of his personal and professional success. His disciplined routine exemplifies how deliberate habits can transform aspirations into achievements.

Modern psychology reinforces the significance of habits in building inner strength. Studies have shown that habits free up cognitive resources by automating routine behaviors, allowing the mind to focus on more complex tasks.

This automation is particularly valuable in times of stress or adversity when decision-making capacity may be compromised. For instance, a person with a habitual practice of journaling or meditating is more likely to turn to these activities during difficult times, using them as tools for clarity and resilience. The consistency of these habits creates a reliable anchor, providing stability amidst uncertainty.

The power of habits lies not only in their consistency but also in their ability to compound over time. James Clear, in his book *Atomic Habits*, describes how small, incremental changes can lead to significant results. He refers to this as the "1% better" principle, emphasizing that improving by just 1% each day leads to exponential growth over time. This concept resonates with historical practices such as the Japanese philosophy of *kaizen*, or continuous improvement. By focusing on gradual progress, individuals can build habits that fortify their inner strength without becoming overwhelmed by the magnitude of their goals.

One of the most critical aspects of habit formation is understanding the interplay between habits and willpower. Contrary to popular belief, willpower is a finite resource, easily depleted by repeated decision-making and self-control. Habits, however, bypass this limitation by embedding desired behaviors into one's routine, reducing reliance on willpower. Consider the example of athletes like Serena Williams, who follow rigorous training schedules with unwavering discipline. Their success is not a product of momentary determination but of habits so ingrained that they become second nature. By creating systems that support their goals, they conserve mental energy for moments that truly demand focus and resilience.

The process of habit formation is as much about removing barriers as it is about adopting new practices. Charles Duhigg, in *The Power of Habit*, explains the habit loop: a cycle of cue, routine, and reward that drives behavior. By understanding this loop, individuals can identify triggers that lead to undesirable habits and replace them with constructive ones. For instance, a person struggling with procrastination might establish a morning routine that includes a specific cue, such as brewing coffee, to signal the start of focused work. Over time, this routine becomes habitual, fostering productivity and reinforcing inner strength.

Historical practices also demonstrate the importance of rituals, which are structured habits imbued with meaning. Religious and cultural rituals, from meditation in Zen Buddhism to the daily prayers of monks, serve as profound examples of how habits can transcend mere functionality to nurture the spirit. These rituals create a sense of purpose and discipline, grounding individuals in their values and fortifying them against life's challenges. The stoics, too, advocated for daily rituals such as journaling and self-reflection, believing that these practices reinforced their philosophical principles and prepared them for adversity.

Practical application of these insights begins with the intentional design of one's environment. Research has shown that the physical and social contexts in which we operate significantly influence habit formation. By arranging one's environment to encourage positive behaviors—placing a journal on the nightstand, for instance, or keeping healthy snacks within reach—individuals can make it easier to adopt habits that support their goals. Similarly, surrounding oneself with supportive peers who share similar values can reinforce the commitment to habit-building, as demonstrated by the success of accountability groups and mentorship programs.

Another critical factor in building strength through habits is patience. Habits are not formed overnight, nor do their benefits manifest immediately. This slow, steady process mirrors the growth of a tree, whose roots deepen and strengthen beneath the surface before its full height is realized. Embracing this gradual progression requires faith in the process and a willingness to endure setbacks. Historical figures like Nelson Mandela exemplify this patience. During his decades of imprisonment, Mandela maintained a daily routine of physical exercise and intellectual engagement, habits that sustained his spirit and prepared him for the leadership role he would later assume.

Ultimately, the role of habits in building strength is both practical and profound. On a practical level, habits simplify life, conserve mental energy, and create a foundation for resilience.

On a deeper level, they shape one's identity, reflecting and reinforcing the values that define a person's character. As readers reflect on their own habits, they are encouraged to consider not only what they do but who they wish to become. By aligning daily actions with long-term aspirations, they can cultivate habits that build inner strength and create a life of purpose and fulfillment.

In the words of Benjamin Franklin, "Energy and persistence conquer all things." This timeless wisdom reminds us that the strength to achieve great things lies not in extraordinary bursts of effort but in the quiet power of consistent, intentional habits. As this section concludes, readers are invited to explore their own routines, recognizing that every small action contributes to the larger journey of self-mastery and success.

Inner Strength as the Pillar of Enduring Success

Enduring success is not an achievement measured solely by accolades or material gains; it is the result of a sustained alignment between purpose, resilience, and emotional well-being.

At its core lies inner strength—the steady force that anchors individuals through triumphs and trials alike. History's most influential minds demonstrate that while external circumstances may shift, those with a solid foundation of inner fortitude possess the clarity and resolve to navigate the complexities of life and emerge stronger.

One of the most enduring examples of inner strength as a cornerstone of success is Abraham Lincoln. Born into poverty, Lincoln faced innumerable hardships, including the deaths of loved ones, business failures, and repeated political defeats. Yet, his unwavering resilience enabled him to become one of America's most revered presidents. Lincoln's leadership during the Civil War was marked by profound emotional strain, yet his ability to remain steadfast in his convictions and empathetic toward both allies and adversaries earned him the respect of a divided nation. His story illustrates that inner strength does not eliminate challenges but equips individuals to persevere in the face of them.

The connection between inner strength and

emotional well-being is equally critical. Emotional well-being is not a state of perpetual
happiness but a balance of mental, emotional,
and spiritual health. Inner strength serves as a
stabilizing force, enabling individuals to manage their emotions constructively and maintain
equilibrium even in difficult times. Consider the
life of Maya Angelou, the acclaimed poet and
activist. Her resilience, born of inner strength,
allowed her to transform personal trauma into
a source of inspiration for others. Angelou's
work demonstrates how emotional well-being
can flourish when grounded in self-awareness,
purpose, and a commitment to growth.

From a philosophical perspective, inner strength
embodies the principle of *areté*, an ancient Greek
concept often translated as "excellence" or "virtue." For the Greeks, *areté* was not a fixed quality
but a lifelong pursuit of fulfilling one's potential. This pursuit required resilience, discipline,
and the courage to confront one's limitations.
Socrates, often considered the father of West-
ern philosophy, emphasized the importance
of self-knowledge as the foundation of inner
strength. "Know thyself," he urged, suggesting
that true success comes from understanding

one's values, strengths, and weaknesses and aligning actions accordingly.

Modern psychology reinforces the idea that inner strength is integral to achieving long-term success. Concepts like grit and resilience have gained prominence as predictors of achievement, often surpassing talent or intelligence in importance. Angela Duckworth, in her book *Grit: The Power of Passion and Perseverance*, argues that sustained success depends on a combination of passion for one's goals and the perseverance to pursue them despite setbacks. This perspective aligns with historical narratives, such as that of Thomas Edison, who famously declared that his failures were merely steps toward eventual success. Edison's ability to view obstacles as opportunities to refine his craft underscores the transformative power of resilience.

The relationship between inner strength and long-term success is also evident in the context of leadership. Leaders who demonstrate composure, empathy, and consistency inspire trust and loyalty, qualities essential for sustained influence. Nelson Mandela exemplified this principle during his presidency in South

Africa. After decades of imprisonment, Mandela emerged not with bitterness but with a vision of reconciliation and unity. His leadership style, rooted in forgiveness and moral courage, highlighted the strength required to prioritize collective well-being over personal grievances. Mandela's legacy is a testament to how inner strength can shape not only individual success but also the progress of entire societies.

Practical applications of inner strength extend beyond extraordinary figures to everyday life. The cultivation of inner strength begins with embracing challenges as opportunities for growth. This mindset, often referred to as an "internal locus of control," emphasizes the belief that individuals have the power to influence their outcomes. While external factors may play a role, those with inner strength focus on what they can control—their thoughts, actions, and attitudes. This proactive approach fosters resilience and empowers individuals to pursue their goals with determination.

Another critical aspect of fostering inner strength is the practice of self-compassion. Unlike self-criticism, which undermines confidence and well-being, self-compassion involves treating oneself with kindness and understanding during times of struggle. Research by psychologist Kristin Neff has shown that self-compassion promotes emotional resilience and reduces feelings of inadequacy. By acknowledging imperfections without judgment, individuals can maintain their motivation and recover more effectively from setbacks. This balance between striving for excellence and accepting one's humanity is a hallmark of enduring success.

Inner strength also requires a commitment to lifelong learning and adaptation. The world is ever-changing, and those who resist growth risk stagnation. This principle is evident in the lives of innovators like Marie Curie, whose groundbreaking work in physics and chemistry was fueled by an insatiable curiosity and resilience in the face of societal and professional barriers. Curie's dedication to continuous learning and her refusal to be deterred by failure exemplify how inner strength enables individuals to thrive in dynamic environments.

Finally, inner strength fosters a sense of purpose that sustains individuals through challenges and triumphs. Viktor Frankl's concept of "logo-therapy," as outlined in *Man's Search for Meaning*, posits that a sense of purpose is essential for resilience and fulfillment. Frankl's experiences in concentration camps revealed that those who found meaning in their suffering—whether through faith, love, or service to others—were more likely to endure. This principle applies broadly to anyone seeking long-term success: by identifying and committing to a purpose greater than oneself, individuals can channel their inner strength toward meaningful and enduring achievements.

As this section concludes, readers are invited to reflect on how inner strength has shaped their own journeys. What challenges have demanded resilience, and how have they grown as a result? By cultivating self-awareness, embracing adversity, and committing to a purpose-driven life, individuals can build the foundation for both success and well-being. Inner strength, as these historical and philosophical insights reveal, is not only a personal asset but a transformative force that ripples outward, influencing families, communities, and even future generations.

In the words of Maya Angelou, "You may encounter many defeats, but you must not be defeated. It may even be necessary to encounter the defeats, so you can know who you are, what you can rise from, how you can still come out of it." These words capture the essence of inner strength as the pillar of enduring success—a quality that enables individuals to rise, again and again, to meet the challenges of life with courage, grace, and determination.

CHAPTER 2: THE VISIONARY MINDSET – SEEING BEYOND THE HORIZON

The Art of Imagination and Creative Thinking

Imagination is the spark of all great achievements. It allows us to see beyond the limitations of the present, to conceive of what could be, and to bring ideas to life. Creative thinking, fueled by imagination, has driven humanity's most significant innovations and transformed the ordinary into the extraordinary. Few figures in history embody the union of imagination and creative genius more profoundly than Leonardo da Vinci. His life and work remain a testament to the power of the visionary mind and the boundless potential of human creativity.

Leonardo da Vinci was more than a painter of masterpieces like the *Mona Lisa* and *The Last Supper*. He was an architect, engineer, inventor, and anatomist—a polymath whose ideas transcended the confines of his era. What set Leonardo apart was his ability to imagine possibilities that others could not yet see. His notebooks, filled with sketches of flying machines, anatomical studies, and complex mechanical devices, reveal a mind unrestrained by conventional boundaries. For Leonardo, imagination

was not idle fantasy but a tool for exploring
the unknown, bridging the gap between what
existed and what could be created.

Leonardo's creative process often began with
observation. He meticulously studied the world
around him, from the flight of birds to the flow
of water. This practice of keen observation laid
the foundation for his imaginative leaps, enabling him to draw connections between seemingly unrelated phenomena. His approach exemplifies the synergy between curiosity and
creativity—an openness to wonder that fuels
imaginative thinking. In his own words, "All
our knowledge has its origin in our perceptions."
By immersing himself in the details of the natural world, Leonardo cultivated a deep reservoir
of insights that informed his groundbreaking
ideas.

Imagination, however, is not limited to the ar-
tistic or scientific realms. It is a universal skill
that can be cultivated and applied to any aspect
of life. Creative thinking allows individuals to
solve problems, adapt to change, and envision
new possibilities. Albert Einstein, another figure
celebrated for his imaginative genius, famously

stated, "Imagination is more important than knowledge. For knowledge is limited, whereas imagination embraces the entire world." Einstein's ability to conceptualize complex theories, such as relativity, stemmed from his willingness to think beyond conventional frameworks, exploring abstract ideas with the same curiosity that Leonardo applied to the natural world.

The art of imagination also involves the courage to challenge assumptions and explore uncharted territory. Visionaries like Leonardo and Einstein were not constrained by the expectations of their time. Instead, they embraced uncertainty and ventured into the unknown, guided by their creative instincts. This willingness to take risks and defy norms is a hallmark of imaginative thinking. It requires resilience in the face of doubt and criticism, as new ideas often provoke skepticism before they are understood or embraced.

Modern psychology sheds light on how imagination can be cultivated and harnessed. Techniques such as "divergent thinking," which involves generating multiple solutions to a problem, encourage the exploration of unconventional ideas. This approach aligns with the brainstorming methods that Leonardo likely employed in his creative endeavors, where he sketched and reimagined concepts from various perspectives. Studies have shown that engaging in activities that stimulate the mind—such as reading fiction, exploring art, or even daydreaming—can enhance creative thinking. These practices foster neural connections that support the generation of novel ideas.

Practical applications of imaginative thinking can begin with curiosity—the practice of asking questions and seeking deeper understanding. Leonardo exemplified this mindset through his insatiable desire to learn. His notebooks are filled with questions like, "Why is the sky blue?" and "How do birds stay aloft?" By cultivating a habit of inquiry, individuals can open their minds to new possibilities and spark creative insights. Curiosity transforms the mundane into the remarkable, encouraging exploration and discovery.

Visualization is another powerful tool for nurturing imagination. Athletes, entrepreneurs, and artists alike use visualization to mentally rehearse their goals and envision success. This technique taps into the brain's ability to simulate experiences, creating a sense of familiarity and confidence that can drive action. Leonardo's sketches of inventions, many of which were centuries ahead of their time, demonstrate how visualization can bring abstract ideas into tangible form. By imagining what does not yet exist, individuals can lay the groundwork for turning their visions into reality.

Imaginative thinking also thrives in environments that encourage experimentation and play. Leonardo's creative process was characterized by a sense of playfulness, evident in his willingness to experiment and take unconventional approaches. This openness to trial and error is essential for innovation, as it allows for the exploration of ideas without fear of failure. In contemporary contexts, fostering a culture of creativity—whether in workplaces, schools, or personal pursuits—can unlock the potential of imaginative thinking.

The art of imagination is not without its challenges. The fear of judgment, the pressure to conform, and the constraints of practicality can stifle creativity. Yet, as history's great visionaries have shown, imagination flourishes when individuals are willing to embrace uncertainty and trust their creative instincts. Leonardo da Vinci's legacy reminds us that the greatest achievements often begin as ideas that defy convention, brought to life by those who dare to dream.

In reflecting on the role of imagination and creative thinking, readers are invited to consider how these principles apply to their own lives. What possibilities remain unexplored, and what questions remain unanswered? By nurturing curiosity, embracing uncertainty, and fostering a sense of play, individuals can unlock their creative potential and develop a visionary mindset. Imagination, as Leonardo demonstrated, is not a rare gift but a skill that can be cultivated through practice and persistence.

As this section concludes, the words of Leonardo da Vinci offer a timeless reminder of the power of imagination: "The noblest pleasure is the joy of understanding." By harnessing the art of creative thinking, individuals can transcend limitations, envision new horizons, and turn their dreams into reality. In doing so, they not only honor the legacy of history's greatest minds but also contribute to the ongoing story of human innovation and achievement.

Foresight and Strategic Planning for the Future

The ability to anticipate and plan for the future is a hallmark of visionary minds. It requires not only imagination but also a structured approach to understanding possibilities, weighing outcomes, and navigating uncertainty. At its core, foresight combines analytical thinking with intuition, enabling individuals to see potential paths and act decisively. Few figures embody this quality as profoundly as Nikola Tesla, whose groundbreaking inventions and visionary ideas revolutionized the modern world.

Nikola Tesla, a Serbian-American inventor, engineer, and futurist, was a master of foresight. His ability to envision technological possibilities years, and sometimes decades, ahead of his time set him apart as one of history's greatest innovators. Tesla imagined wireless communication long before the advent of radio, described concepts akin to the internet, and predicted renewable energy as a cornerstone of society's progress. His foresight was not rooted in fantasy but in a deep understanding of scientific principles and a relentless curiosity about the future's potential.

Tesla's foresight extended beyond individual inventions; he saw connections between technologies and envisioned how they could transform humanity's trajectory. For example, he conceptualized a global wireless energy network that would allow people to transmit power across vast distances without wires—a vision that remains a topic of exploration today. Tesla's ability to anticipate these possibilities stemmed from his unique approach to thinking about the future. He combined a profound understanding of existing systems with an openness to explore what lay beyond their limits.

Strategic planning, the counterpart to foresight, involves translating vision into action. While foresight allows one to see the possibilities, strategic planning is the process of identifying steps to bring those possibilities to fruition. Tesla's meticulous work habits illustrate this balance. He was known to visualize his inventions in extraordinary detail, conducting mental simulations to refine his designs before ever building a prototype. This method of strategic visualization allowed Tesla to bridge the gap between concept and execution with remarkable efficiency.

Foresight and strategic planning are not confined to the realm of scientific innovation. They are essential skills for navigating life's complexities, from personal growth to professional development. Consider the story of Harriet Tubman, whose extraordinary foresight and planning were crucial in her role as a conductor of the Underground Railroad. Tubman's ability to anticipate dangers and devise escape routes enabled her to lead dozens of enslaved individuals to freedom. Her visionary courage and strategic acumen transformed the lives of countless people and left an indelible mark on history.

Philosophically, foresight aligns with the concept of prudence, one of the cardinal virtues in ancient Greek thought. Prudence, or practical wisdom, involves the capacity to deliberate well about what is good and beneficial, considering both present and future implications.

Aristotle described prudence as essential for making sound judgments, emphasizing its role in achieving long-term goals. This perspective underscores the importance of balancing immediate needs with a broader view of the future — a principle that resonates in both personal and professional contexts.

Modern psychology provides valuable insights into the mechanisms of foresight and strategic planning. The concept of mental time travel, for instance, refers to the human capacity to project oneself into the future and imagine potential scenarios. This cognitive ability is crucial for setting goals, evaluating risks, and making informed decisions. Research has shown that individuals who engage in deliberate future-oriented thinking are more likely to achieve their objectives, as they are better equipped to anticipate challenges and devise solutions.

Practical applications of foresight and strategic planning begin with cultivating a mindset of curiosity and inquiry. Tesla's insatiable curiosity drove his explorations, prompting him to ask "what if" and "why not" questions that expanded his understanding of possibilities.

By adopting a similar approach, individuals can open their minds to new perspectives and identify opportunities that might otherwise go unnoticed. Curiosity transforms the unknown into an invitation to explore, laying the groundwork for visionary thinking.

Visualization is another critical tool for fostering foresight. Tesla's mental simulations exemplify how imagining the details of a desired outcome can clarify the steps needed to achieve it. Visualization techniques, such as creating vision boards or mentally rehearsing scenarios, help individuals bridge the gap between abstract goals and actionable plans. These practices enhance clarity, motivation, and focus, making it easier to navigate the complexities of long-term planning.

Strategic planning, in turn, requires breaking down lofty visions into manageable steps. This process involves setting specific, measurable objectives and identifying resources, timelines, and potential obstacles. Tesla's approach to planning his experiments illustrates this principle; he meticulously calculated the parameters of his designs, ensuring that each step brought him closer to his goals. This disciplined approach highlights the importance of combining creativity with structure to turn foresight into tangible results.

One of the most profound lessons from Tesla's life is the value of perseverance in the face of uncertainty. Visionaries often encounter resistance, as their ideas challenge existing paradigms and provoke skepticism. Tesla faced numerous setbacks, from financial struggles to public criticism, yet he remained committed to his vision. His resilience demonstrates that foresight and strategic planning are not guarantees of success but tools for navigating the journey with determination and purpose.

As readers reflect on the themes of foresight and strategic planning, they are encouraged to consider their own futures. What possibilities lie beyond the horizon, and what steps are needed to bring them closer? By embracing curiosity, honing visualization skills, and adopting a strategic approach to planning, individuals can cultivate the visionary mindset exemplified by figures like Nikola Tesla. This mindset enables not only the anticipation of possibilities but also the confidence to pursue them, turning dreams into reality.

In Tesla's words, "The present is theirs; the future, for which I really worked, is mine." This statement encapsulates the essence of foresight and strategic planning—a commitment to shaping the future through vision, action, and perseverance. By adopting these principles, individuals can navigate the uncertainties of life with purpose and clarity, forging a path toward success and fulfillment.

Challenging Conventional Norms to Innovate

Innovation often begins with defiance—a refusal to accept the limitations imposed by tradition, authority, or the status quo. Those who challenge conventional norms do not merely reject established ideas; they see the possibility for something greater, something transformative. History is rich with examples of individuals who broke free from societal expectations and, in doing so, changed the course of human progress. Their stories remind us that innovation thrives where imagination meets courage and where the boundaries of convention are redrawn.

Galileo Galilei stands as a quintessential example of someone who dared to challenge prevailing norms. In the 17th century, the dominant belief in European science was the geocentric model of the universe, which placed Earth at the center of all celestial motion. Galileo, through meticulous observations with his telescope, provided evidence supporting the heliocentric model proposed by Copernicus—a radical idea that placed the Sun at the center of the solar system. By advocating for this paradigm shift, Galileo faced fierce opposition from religious authorities and was eventually placed under house arrest. Yet, his willingness to defy convention paved the way for modern astronomy and reinforced the principle that truth often requires the courage to confront entrenched beliefs.

The process of challenging norms involves more than boldness; it requires a deep understanding of the systems being questioned. Galileo's observations were grounded in empirical evidence, which gave his claims credibility despite their controversy. This combination of intellectual rigor and creative thinking is a hallmark of innovators who successfully disrupt conventions. They approach problems with curiosity, seeking to understand the mechanisms behind accepted practices before proposing alternatives.

Innovation through defiance is not limited to the sciences. In the realm of art, Vincent van Gogh's post-Impressionist works defied the aesthetic norms of his time. While his contemporaries often sought to capture reality with precision, van Gogh used bold colors and expressive brushstrokes to convey emotion and movement. His style, initially dismissed as eccentric, ultimately reshaped the art world and inspired generations of artists to explore new forms of expression. Van Gogh's story underscores that challenging norms is not an act of rebellion for its own sake but a pursuit of authenticity and originality.

Philosophically, the act of challenging conventions aligns with the concept of intellectual humility. Innovators who question norms do so not out of arrogance but out of a recognition that established systems may be incomplete or flawed. Socrates exemplified this principle in ancient Athens, where his method of questioning—known as the Socratic method—encouraged critical examination of commonly held beliefs. By probing the foundations of knowledge, Socrates inspired others to think independently and critically, a legacy that remains central to philosophical inquiry and educational practice.

In the modern era, figures like Steve Jobs have demonstrated the power of challenging conventions in the business world. Jobs's insistence on blending technology with design revolutionized consumer electronics, producing iconic innovations like the iPhone. His approach defied the industry's prevailing focus on functionality alone, instead emphasizing user experience and aesthetic appeal. Jobs famously said, "Innovation distinguishes between a leader and a follower," capturing the essence of his visionary mindset. His story illustrates that challenging norms often requires not only creativity but also an unwavering belief in the value of one's vision.

Psychology sheds light on why challenging norms can be so difficult. Humans are inherently social creatures, and societal norms provide a sense of stability and belonging. Breaking away from these norms can evoke fear of rejection or failure. However, research also shows that stepping outside of one's comfort zone can foster growth and creativity. The willingness to embrace discomfort, whether through experimentation, failure, or criticism, is a critical trait of innovators. This mindset allows individuals to view obstacles not as deterrents but as opportunities for discovery.

Practical applications of this principle begin with fostering a mindset of curiosity and openness. Asking questions such as "Why do we do things this way?" or "What if we tried a different approach?" can lead to new perspectives and insights. This practice of questioning is particularly valuable in environments resistant to change, where established routines may obscure opportunities for improvement. Galileo's telescope, for instance, was not invented to challenge the geocentric model but became a tool for discovery when he asked questions about the stars and planets.

Another key to challenging norms is the willingness to collaborate and learn from diverse perspectives. Innovation often emerges at the intersection of disciplines, where ideas from different fields collide and combine in unexpected ways. The Renaissance itself, of which Galileo was a part, thrived on this interdisciplinary exchange, blending art, science, philosophy, and technology. In contemporary contexts, fostering such cross-disciplinary collaboration can spark creativity and inspire new solutions to complex problems.

Finally, embracing failure as a natural part of the process is essential for challenging norms. Innovators who disrupt conventions often encounter resistance and setbacks, as their ideas challenge deeply held beliefs. Thomas Edison, whose inventions transformed the modern world, famously viewed failure as a stepping stone to success. "I have not failed," he said. "I've just found 10,000 ways that won't work." This perspective highlights the importance of resilience and persistence when pushing the boundaries of what is possible.

As readers reflect on the theme of challenging norms, they are encouraged to consider the conventions that shape their own lives. What assumptions or practices go unquestioned, and what possibilities might emerge by reimagining them? By cultivating curiosity, seeking diverse perspectives, and embracing the courage to defy expectations, individuals can unlock their potential for innovation and creativity.

In the words of Steve Jobs, "The people who are crazy enough to think they can change the world are the ones who do." This sentiment captures the spirit of challenging norms to innovate—a process that begins with a single question and has the power to reshape the future. By daring to see beyond conventional boundaries, individuals can contribute to the legacy of visionaries who have transformed the world through their bold and imaginative thinking.

Adopting a Visionary Mindset in Everyday Life

A visionary mindset is not the exclusive domain of history's great thinkers or trailblazing innovators. While figures like Leonardo da Vinci, Nikola Tesla, and Galileo Galilei may represent the pinnacle of visionary thought, their approach to imagination, foresight, and innovation can be adapted to everyday life. To adopt a visionary mindset is to embrace curiosity, challenge limitations, and consistently look beyond the immediate horizon, cultivating a perspective that transforms the mundane into the extraordinary.

At its core, a visionary mindset begins with curiosity—the drive to ask questions and seek deeper understanding. Albert Einstein once remarked, "I have no special talent. I am only passionately curious." This sentiment underscores that visionary thinking is accessible to anyone willing to cultivate a sense of wonder. Everyday opportunities to ask "why" or "what if" can spark new ideas and inspire creative solutions. For example, someone working in an office might question inefficient workflows and imagine ways to streamline processes, leading to innovations that benefit their entire team. Curiosity is the seed from which all visionary thinking grows, and nurturing it requires openness to exploration and a willingness to see beyond what is immediately apparent.

Another pillar of a visionary mindset is the ability to embrace uncertainty. Visionaries do not shy away from ambiguity; instead, they thrive in it, viewing the unknown as a realm of possibility rather than fear. This mindset can be cultivated in everyday life by reframing challenges as opportunities. Consider the story of Sara Blakely, the founder of Spanx. Faced with frustration over the lack of comfortable undergarments for women, she envisioned a product that didn't yet exist. Blakely's willingness to navigate uncharted territory and her refusal to let uncertainty deter her led to the creation of a billion-dollar brand. Her journey illustrates that the visionary mindset is not about having all the answers but about having the courage to seek them.

Visionaries also excel at connecting the dots between seemingly unrelated ideas, a skill that can be developed through deliberate practice. Steve Jobs, in a famous commencement speech, spoke of how a calligraphy class he took in college influenced the design of Apple's typography and user interface years later. This ability to draw inspiration from diverse experiences is a hallmark of visionary thinking. In everyday life, individuals can adopt this approach by exposing themselves to a variety of disciplines, cultures, and perspectives. Reading widely, attending lectures, or engaging in conversations outside one's usual sphere can foster the creative cross-pollination that fuels innovation.

A practical step toward cultivating a visionary mindset is the practice of visualization. Visionaries like Tesla and Jobs often described their ability to "see" their creations long before they became tangible realities. Visualization is a powerful tool for imagining possibilities and setting goals. Athletes and performers use this technique to mentally rehearse their achievements, creating a sense of confidence and familiarity that translates into success. In daily life, visualization can be applied to personal or professional aspirations, helping individuals clarify their goals and chart a path toward achieving them.

Equally important to the visionary mindset is the practice of resilience. Visionaries often encounter setbacks, skepticism, and even failure. What sets them apart is their ability to persist in the face of these challenges. Resilience is not just about enduring hardship; it is about learning from it and adapting one's approach. Thomas Edison's journey, marked by countless failed experiments before the invention of the light bulb, exemplifies this principle. Edison's perspective—that each failure brought him closer to success—can be adopted in everyday life by viewing setbacks as opportunities for growth rather than as roadblocks.

Mindfulness is another tool that can help cultivate a visionary approach. While visionary thinking often involves looking toward the future, mindfulness anchors individuals in the present moment, fostering clarity and focus. This balance between present awareness and future orientation is essential for turning ideas into reality. For example, a professional working on a complex project can use mindfulness to stay grounded during stressful moments, ensuring that their long-term vision remains clear. Practices like meditation, journaling, or even taking a few minutes each day to reflect can enhance this balance, enabling individuals to think strategically while staying present.

Building a visionary mindset also involves fostering collaboration. Visionaries often surround themselves with diverse, talented individuals who challenge and refine their ideas. Leonardo da Vinci, for instance, was known to engage with thinkers from various disciplines, blending insights from art, science, and engineering. In contemporary life, collaboration can be as simple as seeking feedback from colleagues, participating in group brainstorming sessions, or joining communities of like-minded individuals. These interactions not only enrich one's perspective but also provide the support and accountability needed to bring visionary ideas to fruition.

Lastly, adopting a visionary mindset requires a commitment to action. Visionaries are not merely dreamers; they are doers. The ability to translate ideas into tangible results is what separates visionaries from wishful thinkers. This requires discipline, focus, and a willingness to take calculated risks. In everyday life, this might mean starting a side project, pursuing additional education, or taking small, consistent steps toward a larger goal. By acting on their visions, individuals not only bring their ideas to life but also inspire others to see what is possible.

As readers reflect on these strategies, they are encouraged to consider how they can integrate visionary thinking into their own lives. What questions remain unanswered, and what possibilities remain unexplored? By cultivating curiosity, embracing uncertainty, and taking deliberate action, anyone can develop the habits and mindset of a visionary. Visionary thinking is not confined to history's great figures; it is a skill that can transform ordinary circumstances into extraordinary opportunities.

In the words of Anaïs Nin, "Life shrinks or expands in proportion to one's courage." Adopting a visionary mindset is an act of courage—a decision to see beyond limitations and imagine a brighter future. By embracing this approach, individuals can unlock their potential for growth, creativity, and fulfillment, shaping not only their own lives but also the world around them.

CHAPTER 3: THE ART OF BALANCE – HARMONIZING SUCCESS AND FULFILLMENT

Defining Balance in a Modern Context

In an era defined by relentless speed and unyielding demands, the concept of balance often feels elusive. Yet, throughout history, balance has been revered as a cornerstone of a fulfilling life. From the ancient teachings of Confucius to the modern reflections of psychologists and philosophers, balance has been regarded as the equilibrium between competing forces — a state where ambition and contentment coexist, and where personal and professional spheres harmonize rather than collide.

Balance, however, is not a static achievement. It is a dynamic process, a continuous adjustment to the shifting tides of life. The ancient Greeks captured this idea in the concept of *sophrosyne*, which translates to "moderation" or "temperance." To the Greeks, *sophrosyne* was not merely about avoiding excess; it was about cultivating inner harmony and self-control. Aristotle, one of history's greatest thinkers, emphasized this principle in his doctrine of the "Golden Mean." He argued that virtue lies in finding a balance between extremes — for example, courage exists between recklessness and cowardice, and generosity lies between stinginess and wastefulness. This timeless insight reveals that balance is not about perfection but about seeking the middle path, where strength and stability reside.

The relevance of this ancient wisdom is undeniable in today's fast-paced world. Modern life often demands that individuals juggle multiple roles and responsibilities—career, family, health, and personal aspirations. The pursuit of success frequently tips the scales, leading to burnout, stress, and a sense of disconnection. The philosopher Alain de Botton has observed that modern society tends to celebrate extremes: "We are told we must either work obsessively or escape entirely to find balance, yet true balance lies in integrating the two." His reflection underscores the challenge of defining balance in an age that glorifies overachievement while romanticizing retreat.

The challenge of balance is not unique to our time. Historical figures have grappled with the same tension between ambition and rest, productivity and reflection. Consider the life of Confucius, whose teachings centered on the concept of *zhong yong*, often translated as the "Doctrine of the Mean." This principle advocated for a balanced and harmonious life, rooted in ethical behavior and self-awareness. Confucius believed that balance was achieved through deliberate effort, requiring individuals to cultivate habits that aligned their inner values with their outward actions. His emphasis on moderation and harmony remains profoundly relevant, offering a blueprint for navigating the complexities of modern life.

In addition to historical perspectives, scientific insights shed light on the importance of balance for well-being. Research in psychology and neuroscience has revealed that chronic imbalance—whether from excessive stress or prolonged inactivity—can have detrimental effects on mental and physical health. The concept of work-life balance, for example, has gained prominence as researchers explore the impact of overwork on productivity and happiness. Studies consistently show that individuals who prioritize balance are more likely to experience higher job satisfaction, better relationships, and improved overall health. These findings highlight that balance is not a luxury but a necessity for sustainable success and fulfillment.

The pursuit of balance often begins with self-awareness—an honest examination of one's priorities, values, and habits. Many individuals operate on autopilot, driven by external expectations rather than internal alignment. This lack of intentionality can lead to a life that feels fragmented and unfulfilled. The philosopher Søren Kierkegaard wrote extensively about the concept of the "authentic self," arguing that true fulfillment comes from living in accordance with one's deepest values. To achieve balance, individuals must first identify what matters most to them, discarding distractions and obligations that detract from their core purpose.

Achieving balance also requires a willingness to embrace imperfection. The idea of a perfectly balanced life is a myth, one that often leads to frustration and self-criticism. Instead, balance should be viewed as a flexible and evolving state, one that adapts to changing circumstances. For example, a young professional may prioritize career growth while gradually integrating personal interests and relationships. Later in life, their focus may shift toward family or creative pursuits. This fluid approach to balance acknowledges that life is not a rigid equation but a dynamic interplay of priorities.

Practical strategies for cultivating balance include setting boundaries, practicing mindfulness, and regularly assessing one's commitments. Setting boundaries involves creating space for rest, reflection, and personal growth, even in the midst of demanding schedules. Mindfulness, as both a philosophy and a practice, fosters presence and awareness, helping individuals stay grounded in the moment. Regular self-assessment allows for course corrections, ensuring that one's actions align with their values and goals.

The story of Mahatma Gandhi offers a powerful example of balance in action. Despite his extraordinary activism and political commitments, Gandhi made time for meditation, prayer, and reflection. He believed that inner peace was essential for effective leadership, famously stating, "There is more to life than increasing its speed." Gandhi's life demonstrates that balance is not about doing less but about doing what matters most with intention and focus.

As readers reflect on the idea of balance, they are encouraged to consider how it manifests in their own lives. Are their actions aligned with their values, or are they pulled in conflicting directions? What small adjustments could bring greater harmony to their daily routines? By embracing the wisdom of ancient and modern thinkers, individuals can begin to redefine balance as an ongoing process—a journey toward a more integrated and fulfilling life.

In the words of Rumi, "When the soul lies down in that grass, the world is too full to talk about. Ideas, language, even the phrase each other doesn't make any sense." These poetic lines remind us that balance is not merely about productivity or efficiency but about finding a deeper connection to ourselves and the world around us. By seeking harmony in all aspects of life, we can create a foundation for success and fulfillment that endures the trials of time.

Ambition vs. Contentment: Striking the Right Harmony

Ambition and contentment often seem like opposing forces, pulling individuals in different directions. Ambition drives us to strive for success, push boundaries, and achieve our dreams. Contentment, on the other hand, invites us to appreciate what we have, find joy in the present, and cultivate inner peace. The tension between these two can be challenging to reconcile, yet striking the right harmony between ambition and contentment is essential for sustainable success and fulfillment. History and philosophy offer profound insights into how this balance can be achieved.

Alexander the Great exemplifies the heights of ambition. By the age of 30, he had created one of the largest empires the world had ever seen, driven by an insatiable desire for conquest and legacy. Yet, historical accounts suggest that Alexander struggled with moments of disillusionment, questioning whether his accomplishments could ever bring him true satisfaction. His life serves as a powerful reminder that unchecked ambition, while capable of achieving extraordinary feats, can leave a sense of incompleteness if not tempered by contentment.

In contrast, figures like the Buddha offer a

counterbalance, advocating for the virtues of contentment and moderation. Born Siddhartha Gautama, the Buddha's journey began with the realization that wealth and material success could not provide lasting fulfillment. He sought enlightenment by renouncing worldly attachments and finding inner peace through mindfulness and self-awareness. The Buddha's teachings emphasize that contentment is not about abandoning ambition but about redefining success in terms of inner harmony rather than external achievements.

Philosophically, the tension between ambition and contentment is encapsulated in the concept of *eudaimonia*, a term often translated as "flourishing" or "the good life." Aristotle, a proponent of *eudaimonia*, argued that true fulfillment arises from pursuing excellence while maintaining balance. Ambition, in Aristotle's view, is necessary for achieving one's potential, but it must be guided by reason and virtue to avoid excess. This idea resonates deeply in today's world, where the pursuit of success often overshadows the importance of well-being.

Modern psychology supports the notion that

ambition and contentment are not mutually exclusive but complementary. Research on motivation reveals that individuals with intrinsic goals—those aligned with personal values and passions—are more likely to experience long-term happiness than those driven by extrinsic rewards such as wealth or fame. This insight underscores the importance of aligning ambition with a sense of purpose. When ambition serves a meaningful goal, it can coexist with contentment, creating a sense of fulfillment that is both dynamic and enduring.

Striking this balance requires cultivating a mindset that values both progress and presence. Ambition thrives on forward momentum, while contentment finds joy in the present moment. Reconciling the two involves recognizing that each has its place in the journey of life. Consider the story of Michelle Obama, whose memoir *Becoming* reflects on her journey from ambitious lawyer to First Lady and beyond. Obama's narrative illustrates the importance of embracing both striving and savoring—of setting goals while also appreciating the milestones along the way.

Practical strategies for achieving harmony between ambition and contentment begin with setting clear, meaningful goals. Ambition without direction can lead to burnout, while contentment without purpose may stagnate growth. By identifying aspirations that align with one's values, individuals can channel their energy into pursuits that bring both success and satisfaction. This approach transforms ambition from a source of stress into a driving force for positive change.

Another key to balance is cultivating gratitude. Gratitude fosters contentment by shifting focus from what is lacking to what is present. It does not diminish ambition but provides a foundation of appreciation that enhances resilience and perspective. Regular practices such as journaling about daily blessings or expressing gratitude to others can create a mindset that values progress without becoming consumed by it.

Mindfulness also plays a crucial role in harmonizing ambition and contentment. By fostering awareness of one's thoughts, emotions, and actions, mindfulness helps individuals stay grounded amidst the pursuit of their goals. For example, an entrepreneur driven by ambition might use mindfulness techniques to manage stress, avoid overwork, and remain attuned to the joys of the present. This balance enables sustained productivity and well-being, ensuring that ambition does not come at the cost of health or happiness.

Another example of this balance can be seen in the life of J.R.R. Tolkien, author of *The Lord of the Rings*. Tolkien's ambition drove him to create an expansive fictional universe, a monumental achievement that required years of dedication. Yet, Tolkien also cherished moments of contentment, finding inspiration in quiet walks, friendships, and family life. His ability to integrate ambition with contentment allowed him to sustain his creativity and leave a legacy that continues to inspire millions.

As readers reflect on the interplay between ambition and contentment, they are encouraged to consider how these forces operate in their own lives. Are their ambitions aligned with their values, or are they driven by external pressures? Do they make time to savor their achievements, or are they constantly chasing the next goal? By asking these questions, individuals can begin to redefine success on their own terms, creating a life that balances striving with gratitude, progress with presence.

In the words of Lao Tzu, "Be content with what you have; rejoice in the way things are. When you realize there is nothing lacking, the whole world belongs to you." This ancient wisdom reminds us that contentment is not the absence of ambition but the foundation upon which it rests. By harmonizing ambition with contentment, individuals can achieve not only success but also the fulfillment that makes success worthwhile.

Mindfulness as a Tool for Achieving Harmony

In the cacophony of modern life, mindfulness offers a sanctuary—a way to center oneself amidst the chaos and achieve harmony in mind and spirit. While the term "mindfulness" has gained popularity in recent years, its origins trace back thousands of years to ancient philosophical and spiritual traditions. At its core, mindfulness is the practice of being fully present, observing thoughts and emotions without judgment, and cultivating an awareness of the present moment. This simple yet profound approach has been embraced by philosophers, sages, and leaders throughout history as a tool for achieving balance and emotional equilibrium.

The roots of mindfulness can be found in Buddhist teachings, particularly the practice of *vipassana* or "insight meditation." The Buddha emphasized mindfulness as a path to enlightenment, urging practitioners to observe their thoughts and sensations with clarity and detachment. He described mindfulness as one of the foundational qualities for a balanced life, stating, "Do not dwell in the past, do not dream of the future, concentrate the mind on the present moment." This focus on presence resonates deeply in today's fast-paced world, where distractions abound and the ability to be fully present is often lost amidst the noise.

In addition to its ancient roots, mindfulness has found a place in modern psychology and neuroscience as an evidence-based practice for improving mental and emotional well-being. Dr. Jon Kabat-Zinn, a pioneer in bringing mindfulness to the West, developed Mindfulness-Based

Stress Reduction (MBSR) to help individuals manage stress, anxiety, and chronic pain. His work demonstrated that mindfulness is not merely a spiritual or philosophical concept but a practical tool for navigating the challenges of daily life. Through mindfulness, individuals can develop a greater sense of self-awareness, reduce reactivity, and enhance their ability to respond to situations with intention rather than impulse.

The benefits of mindfulness extend far beyond stress reduction. By cultivating awareness of one's thoughts, emotions, and actions, mindfulness fosters a deeper connection to oneself and the world. This connection is essential for achieving balance, as it allows individuals to recognize when they are veering too far toward extremes—whether in ambition, relationships, or self-care—and make adjustments accordingly. Consider the example of Marcus Aurelius, the Roman emperor and stoic philosopher who practiced a form of mindfulness through his daily reflections. In his journal, which would later be published as *Meditations*, Aurelius wrote, "You have power over your mind—not outside events. Realize this, and you will find strength." His commitment to self-awareness and reflection enabled him to lead with wisdom and maintain equilibrium amidst the pressures of ruling an empire.

Mindfulness also enhances emotional regulation, a key component of harmony. By observing emotions without judgment, individuals can prevent themselves from being swept away by anger, fear, or frustration. This practice creates space between stimulus and response, allowing for more thoughtful and deliberate actions. Viktor Frankl, a Holocaust survivor and psychiatrist, captured this idea in his seminal work *Man's Search for Meaning*. Frankl observed that even in the direst circumstances, individuals retained the freedom to choose their response. This insight underscores the power of mindfulness to transform how we navigate challenges, fostering resilience and inner peace.

Practical applications of mindfulness in achieving harmony begin with simple daily practices. One of the most accessible is mindful breathing—a technique that involves focusing on the rhythm of the breath to anchor the mind in the present. By redirecting attention to the breath, individuals can calm the nervous system, reduce stress, and enhance focus. This practice can be integrated into daily routines, whether as a brief pause during a busy workday or a longer meditation session in the morning or evening.

Another valuable approach is the practice of mindful observation, which involves paying close attention to one's surroundings, thoughts, or emotions without attempting to change them. This practice can be as simple as observing the details of a flower, the sound of rain, or the sensations in the body. By cultivating a sense of curiosity and openness, mindful observation helps individuals break free from autopilot mode and experience life more fully. This heightened awareness fosters a sense of gratitude and contentment, reinforcing the balance between ambition and presence.

Journaling is another powerful tool for mindfulness and reflection. By writing about one's thoughts, feelings, and experiences, individuals can gain clarity and insight into their inner world. This practice aligns with the stoic tradition of daily reflection, as exemplified by Marcus Aurelius. Journaling not only enhances self-awareness but also provides a space for setting intentions and assessing progress toward personal goals.

The integration of mindfulness into daily life also requires a shift in mindset—an intentional effort to prioritize presence over productivity. In a culture that often equates busyness with success, mindfulness serves as a counterbalance, reminding individuals that their worth is not determined by how much they achieve but by the quality of their experiences. This perspective aligns with the teachings of Thich Nhat Hanh, a Vietnamese Zen master and mindfulness advocate, who wrote, "Walk as if you are kissing the Earth with your feet." His words encourage readers to approach life with reverence and intentionality, finding beauty and balance in even the simplest moments.

Mindfulness is not a panacea, nor does it eliminate the challenges of life. However, it equips individuals with the tools to navigate those challenges with greater clarity and composure. By fostering a sense of presence, mindfulness allows individuals to respond to life's demands without becoming overwhelmed, creating space for reflection, connection, and growth.

As readers consider the role of mindfulness in their own lives, they are encouraged to begin with small, intentional steps. What moments in their day could benefit from greater presence? How might mindfulness enhance their ability to balance competing priorities? By incorporating mindfulness practices into their routines, individuals can cultivate the focus and emotional equilibrium needed to achieve harmony in all aspects of life.

In the words of Lao Tzu, "A journey of a thousand miles begins with a single step." Mindfulness invites us to take that step—not toward a distant destination but into the richness of the present moment. By embracing this practice, individuals can transform their relationship with time, rediscover balance, and create a foundation for a life of fulfillment and well-being.

Creating a Life Aligned with Your Values

A life aligned with one's values is a life of authenticity and fulfillment. It is a journey of purpose, where each decision reflects what truly matters to the individual. Yet, in a world of competing demands and external expectations, staying true to one's values requires intentionality and courage. Aligning personal and professional goals with core values is not only essential for achieving balance but also for cultivating a sense of meaning and direction.

The importance of living in alignment with one's values is echoed throughout history and philosophy. Socrates famously declared, "An unexamined life is not worth living," emphasizing the need for self-reflection and an understanding of one's guiding principles. For Socrates, values were the foundation of a virtuous life, influencing how one thought, acted, and interacted with others. His philosophy reminds us that values are not abstract ideals but practical guides that shape our decisions and relationships.

This concept is exemplified in the life of Mahatma Gandhi, whose unwavering commitment to nonviolence and truth guided his actions as a leader and activist. Gandhi's principle of *ahimsa*—the practice of non-harm—was not just a moral stance but a value that permeated every aspect of his life. From organizing peaceful protests to engaging in self-discipline, Gandhi demonstrated how aligning actions with values can create profound personal and societal change. His life serves as a reminder that values provide a compass, even in the face of adversity, enabling individuals to stay grounded and focused on what truly matters.

Aligning one's life with core values begins with clarity. Many individuals drift through life without fully understanding what drives them, adopting goals and behaviors shaped by societal expectations or external pressures. However, true fulfillment arises from within, rooted in an authentic understanding of one's values. The philosopher Friedrich Nietzsche spoke of the "will to power," not as a pursuit of domination but as the drive to live authentically and fulfill one's potential. For Nietzsche, this required rejecting superficial norms and embracing the values that resonated with one's deepest self.

The process of identifying values involves introspection and reflection. Journaling, meditation, and honest conversations with trusted confidants can reveal the principles that resonate most strongly. For example, an individual might discover that they value creativity, compassion, and freedom. These values then become a framework for evaluating decisions, ensuring that goals and actions align with what is most meaningful. This alignment fosters a sense of coherence and purpose, reducing inner conflict and enhancing overall well-being.

Once values are identified, the challenge lies in integrating them into daily life. This requires bridging the gap between intention and action—a task that demands discipline, awareness, and adaptability. Viktor Frankl, in his seminal work *Man's Search for Meaning*, described how even in the harrowing conditions of a concentration camp, individuals could find meaning by holding steadfast to their values. For Frankl, values such as love, faith, and hope provided the strength to endure and a sense of purpose amidst suffering. His insights reveal that values are not theoretical constructs but powerful tools for navigating life's challenges.

One practical strategy for aligning life with values is setting goals that reflect those values. For instance, an individual who values connection might prioritize spending quality time with loved ones or building meaningful relationships in their professional life. Similarly, someone who values growth may seek out opportunities for learning and development, ensuring that their personal and professional paths align with their desire for progress. By linking goals to values, individuals can create a roadmap that guides their decisions and actions.

Another critical aspect of alignment is the ability to say no to distractions and commitments that conflict with one's values. In a culture that often glorifies busyness, the courage to set boundaries is essential for preserving integrity and focus. This principle is evident in the life of Steve Jobs, who famously emphasized the importance of saying no to countless opportunities in order to concentrate on what mattered most. Jobs's commitment to simplicity and excellence allowed him to align Apple's mission with his vision, creating products that reflected his core values of design, innovation, and user experience.

Mindfulness can also play a vital role in maintaining alignment with values. By fostering awareness of one's thoughts, emotions, and behaviors, mindfulness helps individuals stay attuned to their intentions and avoid being swayed by external pressures. For example, a professional facing a difficult decision might use mindfulness techniques to pause, reflect on their values, and choose a course of action that aligns with their principles. This practice not only enhances decision-making but also strengthens the connection between values and actions.

Aligning life with values is not a one-time effort but an ongoing process. As individuals grow and evolve, their understanding of their values may deepen, and their goals may shift accordingly. Regular reflection and reassessment are essential for ensuring that one's life remains aligned with what is truly meaningful. This dynamic process allows individuals to adapt to changing circumstances while staying true to their core principles.

The rewards of living in alignment with values are profound. Individuals who prioritize authenticity and purpose often experience greater resilience, as their actions are rooted in a sense of meaning that transcends temporary setbacks. They are also more likely to cultivate fulfilling relationships, as their interactions are guided by integrity and mutual respect. Moreover, aligning personal and professional goals with values creates a sense of harmony, reducing the tension between competing priorities and fostering a balanced and integrated life.

As readers reflect on this chapter, they are encouraged to consider their own values and how they influence their decisions. What principles guide their actions, and how well do their current goals align with those principles? By taking the time to explore these questions, individuals can begin the journey toward a life that reflects their deepest convictions.

In the words of Ralph Waldo Emerson, "To be yourself in a world that is constantly trying to make you something else is the greatest accomplishment." Living in alignment with one's values is an act of authenticity and courage—a commitment to pursuing a life of purpose, balance, and fulfillment. By embracing this path, individuals can create a legacy that resonates not only with their own hearts but with the world around them.

CHAPTER 4: THE POWER OF PERSISTENCE – OVERCOMING OBSTACLES

Understanding the Psychology of Persistence

Persistence is the driving force behind many of history's greatest achievements. It is the capacity to sustain effort and commitment in the face of difficulty, to push forward despite setbacks, and to believe in the eventual realization of a goal. While talent and opportunity are often credited for success, persistence remains the common denominator among those who overcome adversity to achieve their dreams. At its core, persistence is not merely an action but a mindset—a psychological framework that transforms obstacles into opportunities.

Thomas Edison, one of the most prolific inventors in history, exemplifies the power of persistence. Over his lifetime, Edison accumulated more than 1,000 patents, including those for the phonograph, motion picture camera, and incandescent light bulb. Yet, his path to success was far from smooth. Edison famously conducted thousands of experiments before perfecting the light bulb. Reflecting on this process, he remarked, "I have not failed. I've just found 10,000 ways that won't work." This perspective reveals the essence of persistence: a willingness to learn from failure, adapt strategies, and maintain an unwavering belief in the possibility of success.

Psychologically, persistence is deeply tied to motivation and resilience. Motivation provides the initial spark to pursue a goal, while resilience sustains the effort needed to achieve it. Research in psychology identifies two primary types of motivation: intrinsic and extrinsic. Intrinsic motivation arises from within, driven by personal interest or the satisfaction of achieving a goal. Extrinsic motivation, on the other hand, is influenced by external rewards such as recognition, money, or status. While both forms of motivation can fuel persistence, intrinsic motivation is often more enduring, as it aligns with an individual's values and passions.

The connection between resilience and persistence is equally critical. Resilience, often described as the ability to bounce back from setbacks, enables individuals to maintain their commitment to a goal even when progress seems slow or uncertain. Viktor Frankl, a Holocaust survivor and psychiatrist, wrote extensively about this relationship in *Man's Search for*

Meaning. Frankl observed that individuals who found meaning in their suffering were more likely to persevere, even in the most harrowing circumstances. His insights underscore that persistence is not just a physical effort but a mental and emotional one, rooted in a sense of purpose.

Historical and modern examples of persistence reveal that setbacks are not failures but stepping stones. Consider J.K. Rowling, the author of the *Harry Potter* series. Before achieving global fame, Rowling faced rejection from multiple publishers, financial hardship, and personal struggles. However, her persistence and belief in her story eventually led to the creation of a literary phenomenon that has inspired millions. Rowling's journey demonstrates that persistence often involves redefining success, viewing each setback as a temporary detour rather than a permanent roadblock.

The psychology of persistence is also influenced by one's mindset. Carol Dweck, a renowned psychologist, introduced the concept of the "growth mindset" to describe the belief that abilities and intelligence can be developed through effort and learning. Individuals with a growth mindset view challenges as opportunities for growth, which fosters persistence. In contrast, a fixed mindset—believing that abilities are innate and unchangeable—can lead to avoidance of challenges and a tendency to give up when faced with obstacles. Cultivating a growth mindset is therefore essential for sustaining persistence over the long term.

Practical applications of persistence begin with setting meaningful and achievable goals. Goals provide a sense of direction and purpose, acting as a north star that guides effort and focus. However, not all goals are created equal. Research shows that goals aligned with an individual's values and passions are more likely to inspire persistence. For example, an aspiring entrepreneur driven by a desire to create positive social change may find it easier to persevere through challenges than someone pursuing a goal solely for financial gain.

Another critical aspect of persistence is the ability to reframe failure. Edison's perspective on his experiments reflects a powerful mental shift: seeing failure not as an endpoint but as valuable feedback. This reframing reduces the emotional burden of setbacks and encourages individuals to continue their efforts with renewed determination. For instance, an athlete training for a marathon might view a slower-than-expected time as an opportunity to adjust their training regimen rather than as evidence of inadequacy.

Support systems also play a significant role in fostering persistence. Surrounding oneself with supportive friends, mentors, or colleagues can provide encouragement and accountability during challenging times. For example, the Wright brothers, pioneers of aviation, relied on each other's support and shared determination as they worked to achieve human flight. Their persistence, fueled by mutual encouragement and collaboration, ultimately changed the course of history.

Mindfulness practices can further enhance persistence by fostering focus and emotional regulation. When faced with setbacks, mindfulness helps individuals stay present, reducing the tendency to ruminate on past failures or worry about future uncertainties. This focus allows for a clearer assessment of the situation and a more intentional response. A professional navigating a complex project, for example, might use mindfulness techniques to maintain clarity and resilience, enabling them to persist despite obstacles.

Ultimately, the psychology of persistence is a testament to the power of belief, effort, and adaptability. It reminds us that success is rarely a straight path but a journey marked by twists, turns, and moments of doubt. By understanding the factors that drive persistence—motivation, resilience, mindset, and support—individuals can cultivate this essential quality and apply it to their own lives.

As readers reflect on this section, they are encouraged to consider how persistence has played a role in their own achievements. What challenges have they faced, and how did they overcome them? By embracing the lessons of figures like Edison, Rowling, and Frankl, individuals can begin to see obstacles not as barriers but as opportunities to grow stronger and more determined.

In the words of Calvin Coolidge, "Nothing in this world can take the place of persistence.

Talent will not; nothing is more common than unsuccessful men with talent. Genius will not; unrewarded genius is almost a proverb. Education will not; the world is full of educated derelicts. Persistence and determination alone are omnipotent." This enduring wisdom reminds us that the ability to keep going, to persist through challenges, is one of the most powerful forces for achieving success and fulfillment.

Transforming Failure into Growth Opportunities

Failure is often perceived as the antithesis of success—a barrier that halts progress and diminishes confidence. Yet, for those who achieve greatness, failure is not an endpoint but a stepping stone. The ability to view failure as feedback and leverage it as a catalyst for growth is a defining trait of resilient and successful individuals. History is replete with stories of people who embraced their failures, learned from them, and emerged stronger, demonstrating that setbacks are not to be feared but to be transformed.

One of the most compelling examples of turning failure into opportunity is the story of Thomas

Edison's invention of the electric light bulb. Edison's thousands of failed experiments were not viewed as defeats but as essential steps in his journey. When questioned about his repeated failures, Edison famously replied, "I have not failed. I've just found 10,000 ways that won't work." This reframing of failure as a process of discovery underscores the mindset that enables growth. Each misstep provided Edison with valuable insights, guiding him closer to the solution. His persistence and perspective exemplify the power of seeing failure not as a reflection of one's limitations but as an integral part of innovation.

The transformative potential of failure lies in its ability to reveal areas for improvement. Every setback offers an opportunity to reflect, adapt, and refine one's approach. Consider the case of Sara Blakely, the founder of Spanx. Before building her billion-dollar brand, Blakely experienced numerous setbacks, including rejection from law schools and struggles in her early sales career. However, she credits her success to her willingness to embrace failure. Blakely often recounts how her father encouraged her to discuss her failures at the dinner table, framing them as opportunities for learning and growth. This perspective allowed her to approach challenges with curiosity and resilience, ultimately leading to her groundbreaking innovation in the fashion industry.

Philosophically, the concept of failure as a growth opportunity aligns with the teachings of stoicism. Stoic philosophers like Epictetus emphasized that obstacles are not inherently negative but are shaped by one's perception. In his work *Discourses*, Epictetus wrote, "It's not what happens to you, but how you react to it that matters." This insight highlights the importance of mindset in navigating failure. By reframing setbacks as learning experiences, individuals can maintain their composure and focus, using failure as a tool for self-improvement rather than a source of despair.

Modern psychology reinforces the idea that failure can be a powerful motivator for growth. The concept of "productive failure," studied by researchers in education and cognitive science, demonstrates that struggling with a problem before finding a solution enhances learning and retention. This principle is evident in the practice of deliberate practice, a technique used by experts in various fields to improve their skills. Deliberate practice involves identifying weaknesses, making mistakes, and correcting them through focused effort. This process mirrors the broader journey of transforming failure into growth, where missteps become opportunities for refinement.

The ability to transform failure into growth opportunities also requires emotional resilience. Resilience is not about avoiding negative emotions but about managing them constructively. For example, Michael Jordan, widely regarded as one of the greatest basketball players of all time, famously said, "I've missed more than 9,000 shots in my career. I've lost almost 300 games. Twenty-six times I've been trusted to take the game-winning shot and missed. I've failed over and over and over again in my life. And that is why I succeed." Jordan's ability to channel disappointment into motivation exemplifies how resilience enables individuals to persevere and learn from failure.

Practical strategies for leveraging failure begin with self-reflection. Taking the time to analyze what went wrong, without self-criticism or blame, allows individuals to identify actionable lessons. Journaling or discussing failures with a trusted mentor can provide clarity and perspective, transforming setbacks into valuable learning experiences. For instance, an entrepreneur whose business venture did not succeed might reflect on market dynamics, operational challenges, or leadership decisions, using these insights to inform future endeavors.

Another key strategy is adopting a growth mindset, a concept popularized by psychologist Carol Dweck. A growth mindset views abilities and intelligence as malleable, emphasizing the value of effort and persistence. Individuals with this mindset see failure not as a judgment of their worth but as a necessary part of the learning process. This perspective encourages experimentation, creativity, and resilience, enabling individuals to approach challenges with confidence and adaptability.

Support systems also play a critical role in transforming failure into growth. Surrounding oneself with supportive and understanding peers, mentors, or colleagues creates an environment where failures are viewed as opportunities rather than shortcomings. Consider the example of NASA's Apollo program, where engineers and scientists collaborated to learn from their mistakes during the early stages of space exploration. Each failure, from launchpad explosions to mission aborts, was meticulously analyzed, leading to the eventual success of the Apollo 11 moon landing. The culture of learning and collaboration within the program demonstrates how collective reflection can turn setbacks into groundbreaking achievements.

Additionally, cultivating patience and persistence is essential for navigating the emotional and practical challenges of failure. Success often requires repeated attempts, each informed by the lessons of previous efforts. J.K. Rowling, who faced rejection from multiple publishers before the *Harry Potter* series became a global phenomenon, exemplifies this principle. Her story underscores the importance of perseverance in the face of discouragement, illustrating that failure is often a precursor to success.

As readers reflect on the role of failure in their own lives, they are encouraged to consider how setbacks have shaped their growth. What lessons have been learned, and how have these experiences influenced their goals and strategies? By viewing failure as feedback, individuals can begin to see challenges not as barriers but as opportunities to refine their skills, deepen their understanding, and strengthen their resolve.

In the words of Winston Churchill, "Success is not final, failure is not fatal: It is the courage to continue that counts." This sentiment captures the essence of transforming failure into growth opportunities. By embracing failure as an inevitable and valuable part of the journey, individuals can unlock their potential, achieving not only their goals but also the resilience and wisdom that come from overcoming adversity.

Developing Emotional Resilience Through Setbacks

Resilience is the ability to withstand and recover from adversity—a quality that lies at the heart of persistence. While challenges and setbacks are inevitable, emotional resilience allows individuals to adapt, learn, and continue moving forward. This capacity is not an inherent trait but a skill that can be developed, as exemplified by figures like Helen Keller, who overcame profound challenges to achieve greatness. Her life story serves as a testament to the power of resilience, offering timeless lessons on navigating difficulties with courage and determination.

Helen Keller's early life was marked by profound adversity. At just 19 months old, she lost her sight and hearing due to an illness, leaving her isolated in a world of silence and darkness. Yet, through her resilience and the support of her teacher, Anne Sullivan, Keller defied expectations. She learned to communicate, graduated from Radcliffe College, and became an author, activist, and speaker. Keller's achievements were not the result of overcoming her disabilities alone but of transforming them into sources of strength. Her ability to persist through challenges, fueled by emotional resilience, enabled her to inspire millions and advocate for social change.

The foundation of Keller's resilience was her mindset. Rather than dwelling on what she had lost, she focused on what she could achieve. This perspective aligns with the principles of positive psychology, which emphasize the importance of reframing challenges as opportunities for growth. By shifting focus from limitations to possibilities, Keller exemplified how resilience begins with a choice—a decision to confront difficulties with optimism and determination.

One of the most powerful aspects of Keller's resilience was her ability to find meaning in her experiences. Viktor Frankl, a Holocaust survivor and psychiatrist, wrote extensively about the relationship between meaning and resilience in his book *Man's Search for Meaning*. Frankl argued that even in the face of unimaginable suffering, individuals could endure by finding purpose. Keller embodied this principle, channeling her struggles into advocacy for disability rights, education, and social justice. Her life demonstrates that resilience is not merely about enduring hardship but about using it to create a positive impact.

The development of emotional resilience involves cultivating self-awareness and emotional regulation. Resilient individuals are not immune to negative emotions but are skilled at managing them constructively. For example, when Keller encountered frustration or setbacks in her education, she relied on strategies such as deep breathing, reflective writing, and open communication with Sullivan to process her emotions. These practices enabled her to maintain her focus and composure, even in the face of significant challenges.

Historical and contemporary examples further illustrate the power of resilience in achieving greatness. Nelson Mandela, who endured 27 years of imprisonment during South Africa's apartheid era, maintained his resolve through a deep sense of purpose and forgiveness. Mandela's ability to navigate immense suffering without bitterness exemplifies the strength that comes from emotional resilience. Like Keller, Mandela found meaning in his experiences, using them as a platform for promoting reconciliation and equality.

Resilience is also deeply connected to the concept of grit, popularized by psychologist Angela Duckworth. Grit encompasses passion and perseverance toward long-term goals, even in the face of setbacks. Duckworth's research highlights that resilience is a key component of grit, enabling individuals to sustain effort and commitment despite obstacles. Keller's determination to learn language—a goal that required immense patience and persistence—reflects the interplay between grit and resilience. Her triumph in mastering communication underscores that resilience is not about avoiding hardship but about embracing the process of overcoming it.

Developing emotional resilience requires intentional effort and practice. One effective approach is to build a support network of trusted individuals who provide encouragement, guidance, and perspective during challenging times. Keller's relationship with Anne Sullivan illustrates the transformative power of mentorship and support. Sullivan's unwavering belief in Keller's potential, combined with her innovative teaching methods, played a crucial role in Keller's journey. This partnership highlights the importance of surrounding oneself with people who uplift and inspire resilience.

Another critical aspect of resilience is self-compassion. Resilient individuals treat themselves with kindness and understanding, especially during moments of failure or disappointment. This practice reduces self-criticism and fosters a sense of self-worth, creating a solid foundation for perseverance. Keller's acceptance of her limitations, coupled with her determination to rise above them, reflects the balance between self-compassion and ambition that characterizes emotional resilience.

Mindfulness is another valuable tool for developing resilience. By fostering awareness of the present moment, mindfulness helps individuals navigate stress and uncertainty with greater clarity and calm. For example, a professional facing a high-pressure deadline might use mindfulness techniques to manage anxiety and maintain focus, enabling them to approach the task with resilience. This practice not only enhances emotional regulation but also strengthens the ability to adapt to changing circumstances.

As readers reflect on Keller's story and the broader concept of emotional resilience, they are encouraged to consider their own approaches to adversity. How do they respond to setbacks, and what strategies might help them navigate challenges more effectively? By cultivating resilience through self-awareness, support networks, and purposeful action, individuals can transform difficulties into opportunities for growth and achievement.

In the words of Helen Keller, "Although the world is full of suffering, it is also full of the overcoming of it." Her life is a testament to the boundless potential of the human spirit, reminding us that resilience is not the absence of struggle but the ability to rise above it. By embracing this perspective, individuals can develop the emotional strength to face life's challenges with grace, determination, and hope.

Practical Strategies for Cultivating Unwavering Persistence

Persistence is the engine of achievement. It powers progress, carries individuals through setbacks, and ensures that dreams are pursued with unwavering determination. While the concept of persistence often evokes images of grand feats and historical triumphs, it is equally vital in everyday life, from navigating personal challenges to achieving professional goals. Cultivating persistence is not a matter of sheer willpower alone—it is a deliberate process that involves strategies, mindset shifts, and the cultivation of supportive habits.

A powerful starting point for building persistence is to set clear, meaningful goals. Without a sense of direction, effort can feel aimless and exhausting. Clarity of purpose provides the motivation needed to persist through difficulties, as seen in the life of Florence Nightingale, the founder of modern nursing. Nightingale's goal of improving healthcare systems drove her relentless efforts during the Crimean War and beyond. Her clear vision allowed her to endure opposition, illness, and exhaustion, transforming her setbacks into stepping stones. Nightingale's story underscores the importance of defining a purpose that resonates deeply, providing a wellspring of motivation even in the face of adversity.

In addition to goal setting, breaking down objectives into manageable steps is an essential strategy for sustaining persistence. Large goals can feel overwhelming, leading to procrastination or burnout. By dividing a goal into smaller, achievable milestones, individuals can maintain a sense of progress and momentum. Consider the story of Nelson Mandela, whose goal of ending apartheid required decades of effort. During his 27 years of imprisonment, Mandela focused on small but meaningful actions, such as educating fellow prisoners and building relationships with his captors. These incremental steps ultimately contributed to his larger vision of a free and equal South Africa. Mandela's approach illustrates that persistence is often fueled by celebrating small victories along the way.

Another critical element of persistence is the cultivation of self-discipline. Discipline provides the structure and consistency needed to sustain effort over time. James Clear, author of *Atomic Habits*, emphasizes the role of habits in achieving long-term success. According to Clear, persistence is not about relying on bursts of motivation but about creating systems that make progress inevitable. For example, an aspiring writer might establish a daily writing routine, committing to a specific word count regardless of inspiration. Over time, these habits build momentum and resilience, making it easier to persist even during challenging periods.

A growth mindset, popularized by psychologist Carol Dweck, is another cornerstone of unwavering persistence. Individuals with a growth mindset view challenges as opportunities to learn and grow, rather than as indicators of failure. This perspective fosters resilience and adaptability, enabling individuals to approach obstacles with curiosity and determination. Historical figures like Thomas Edison exemplify this mindset, embracing failures as part of the creative process. By adopting a growth-oriented perspective, individuals can maintain their persistence even when faced with setbacks.

Support systems also play a vital role in sustaining persistence. Surrounding oneself with encouraging and like-minded individuals creates a network of accountability and inspiration. This principle is evident in the story of the Wright brothers, whose collaborative efforts led to the invention of the airplane. Wilbur and Orville Wright supported each other through countless experiments, failures, and challenges, drawing strength from their shared vision. Similarly, individuals can enhance their persistence by seeking mentors, joining communities, or forming partnerships that provide encouragement and constructive feedback.

Resilience, a close ally of persistence, can be strengthened through practices such as mindfulness and self-compassion. Mindfulness fosters present-moment awareness, reducing the tendency to dwell on setbacks or worry about future challenges. Self-compassion, on the other hand, allows individuals to treat themselves with kindness during moments of difficulty, reducing self-criticism and fostering a sense of emotional balance. Together, these practices create a foundation of inner strength that supports persistent effort. For example, a professional facing a challenging project might use mindfulness to stay focused and self-compassion to navigate moments of doubt, enabling them to persevere with clarity and confidence.

Reframing failure is another powerful strategy for cultivating persistence. Failure is an inevitable part of any meaningful endeavor, but it does not have to be a source of discouragement. Instead, it can be viewed as valuable feedback—a natural part of the learning process. The story of J.K. Rowling, who faced numerous rejections before publishing the *Harry Potter* series, highlights this principle. Rowling's ability to persist through setbacks stemmed from her belief in her work and her willingness to learn from rejection. By viewing failure as a stepping stone rather than a roadblock, individuals can maintain their persistence and continue striving toward their goals.

Flexibility is another key component of persistence. While determination is essential, rigidity can lead to burnout or wasted effort. Being willing to adapt strategies, revise goals, or explore alternative paths allows individuals to navigate obstacles more effectively. For example, when faced with limited resources, entrepreneurs like Elon Musk have pivoted their approaches, finding innovative solutions to achieve their objectives. This adaptability ensures that persistence is not about stubbornness but about sustained and intelligent effort.

Finally, the practice of visualization can reinforce persistence by keeping the desired outcome vivid and tangible. Visualization involves imagining the successful completion of a goal, along with the steps required to achieve it. Athletes, artists, and entrepreneurs alike use this technique to maintain focus and motivation. For instance, Olympic athletes often mentally rehearse their performances, creating a sense of familiarity and confidence that drives their persistence. In daily life, individuals can use visualization to stay connected to their aspirations, reinforcing their commitment to overcome challenges.

As readers reflect on these strategies, they are encouraged to consider how they can integrate persistence into their own lives. What goals inspire them to push forward, and what practices can support their journey? By cultivating habits, mindset shifts, and support systems, individuals can build the resilience and determination needed to achieve their dreams.

In the words of Calvin Coolidge, "Press on. Nothing in the world can take the place of persistence." This enduring wisdom reminds us that persistence is not about perfection but about perseverance. By embracing practical strategies and maintaining a steadfast commitment to their goals, individuals can harness the power of persistence to overcome obstacles, achieve success, and create a life of fulfillment and purpose.

CHAPTER 5: LEADERSHIP AND INFLUENCE – GUIDING WITH PURPOSE

The Essence of Purposeful Leadership

Leadership is not merely about wielding authority or achieving goals—it is about inspiring
others to strive for a shared vision and fostering
unity in the pursuit of something greater than
oneself. At its heart, leadership is an act of service, driven by purpose and guided by values.
Purposeful leadership has the power to transform individuals and communities, creating a
ripple effect that transcends time and space. Few
figures embody this concept as profoundly as
Mahatma Gandhi, whose life and work serve as
a masterclass in leading with purpose.

Mahatma Gandhi's leadership emerged during
one of the most tumultuous periods in India's
history. Faced with colonial oppression and
widespread social injustices, Gandhi rallied
millions of people to fight for independence
through nonviolent resistance. His philosophy
of *ahimsa* (nonviolence) and *satyagraha* (truth
force) became the bedrock of his leadership,
emphasizing moral conviction and the power
of collective action. Gandhi's ability to inspire
and unite people was rooted in his unwavering
commitment to a higher purpose: the liberation

and dignity of his fellow countrymen.

The foundation of purposeful leadership lies in clarity of purpose. Gandhi's vision for an independent and equitable India was not just a political ambition—it was a moral imperative. This clarity allowed him to navigate challenges with steadfastness, even when faced with imprisonment, violence, and personal sacrifice. Purposeful leaders, like Gandhi, understand that their role is not to dominate but to elevate, to align their actions with a mission that resonates deeply with their values and inspires those around them.

A key aspect of Gandhi's leadership was his ability to lead by example. He lived simply, wearing traditional Indian clothing, practicing self-discipline, and embracing humility. This authenticity fostered trust and respect among his followers, who saw in Gandhi a leader who embodied the principles he espoused. His approach underscores an essential truth about leadership: it is not just about what one says, but about how one lives. Purposeful leadership requires integrity—a consistency between one's values, words, and actions that inspires confidence and loyalty.

The essence of purposeful leadership also lies in the ability to connect with people on an emotional and moral level. Gandhi's leadership was not built on coercion or fear but on a shared sense of humanity and justice. He understood the power of storytelling, using anecdotes and parables to communicate complex ideas in a way that resonated with ordinary people. By framing his vision in terms of universal values—freedom, equality, and nonviolence—Gandhi created a movement that transcended political divisions and united people across social, religious, and cultural boundaries.

Philosophically, purposeful leadership aligns with the concept of servant leadership, popularized by Robert K. Greenleaf in the 20th century. A servant leader prioritizes the needs of others, fostering their growth and well-being while pursuing collective goals. Gandhi's leadership exemplified this philosophy, as he consistently placed the welfare of his people above his own interests. His humility and willingness to endure hardship for the sake of others created a model of leadership that continues to inspire movements for social change worldwide.

Modern psychology also offers insights into the qualities that define purposeful leadership. Research on transformational leadership high-lights the importance of vision, inspiration, and individual consideration. Transformational leaders, like Gandhi, inspire others by articu-lating a compelling vision of the future, motivat-ing them to transcend their self-interest for the greater good. This approach fosters a sense of purpose and belonging, empowering individu-als to contribute their talents and energy toward a common goal.

Practical applications of purposeful leadership begin with self-reflection. Leaders must ask themselves: What is my purpose? What values guide my actions? By cultivating self-awareness, individuals can clarify their motivations and align their leadership style with their core prin-ciples. For example, a manager leading a team might reflect on how their decisions impact not only productivity but also the well-being and development of their team members. This introspection creates a foundation for authentic and purpose-driven leadership.

Another essential practice is active listening. Purposeful leaders understand that leadership is a dialogue, not a monologue. By listening to the needs, concerns, and aspirations of their followers, leaders can build trust and foster collaboration. Gandhi's willingness to listen to diverse perspectives within the Indian independence movement allowed him to navigate internal conflicts and maintain unity. Similarly, modern leaders can strengthen their teams by creating an environment where every voice is valued and heard.

Purposeful leadership also requires the courage to make difficult decisions. Gandhi's commitment to nonviolence often placed him in opposition to those who advocated for more aggressive tactics. Yet, he remained resolute, guided by his principles rather than by expedience or popular opinion. This courage to stand by one's convictions, even when it is challenging or unpopular, is a hallmark of purposeful leadership. It demonstrates to others that the leader's actions are grounded in integrity, earning their respect and loyalty.

Finally, purposeful leadership involves cultivating a sense of shared ownership. Gandhi's movement was not about him—it was about the people he served. By empowering individuals to take ownership of the struggle for independence, he transformed a movement into a collective endeavor. Modern leaders can adopt this approach by fostering a culture of collaboration and empowerment, ensuring that every individual feels invested in the mission and its outcomes.

As readers reflect on the essence of purposeful leadership, they are invited to consider how these principles apply to their own lives. What purpose drives their actions, and how can they align their leadership style with their values? By embracing the lessons of figures like Gandhi, individuals can cultivate leadership that not only achieves results but also inspires and uplifts those they lead.

In the words of Mahatma Gandhi, "The best way to find yourself is to lose yourself in the service of others." This timeless wisdom reminds us that leadership is not about seeking power but about serving with purpose. By leading with integrity, empathy, and vision, individuals can create a legacy of meaningful impact, guiding others toward a brighter and more united future.

Leading with Integrity and Authenticity

Leadership rooted in integrity and authenticity possesses a transformative power that inspires trust, loyalty, and resilience. At its core, such leadership transcends superficial authority, fostering meaningful connections through honesty and consistent alignment with values. Throughout history, figures like Winston Churchill have exemplified the profound impact of leading with integrity and authenticity, navigating turbulent times with unwavering commitment to their principles and a deep sense of responsibility.

Winston Churchill, the indomitable British Prime Minister during World War II, is celebrated for his steadfast leadership during one of history's darkest hours. At a time when Britain faced existential threats from Nazi Germany, Churchill's authenticity and integrity became beacons of hope. He did not sugarcoat the challenges ahead; instead, he addressed the British people with candor and resolve. His speeches, such as the iconic "We shall fight on the beaches" address, reflected an unvarnished truth about the gravity of the situation, paired with an un-yielding determination to prevail. This honesty earned him the trust of a nation, galvanizing them to endure hardship and unite in pursuit of victory.

Churchill's leadership style was deeply authen-tic because it reflected his unique character and convictions. He was unapologetically himself— bold, eloquent, and unafraid to take unpopular stances when he believed they were right. For example, his warnings about the rise of Adolf Hitler and the need for rearmament were met with skepticism and criticism in the years lead-ing up to the war. Yet, Churchill remained reso-lute, guided by his principles rather than public opinion. His authenticity, combined with his ability to articulate a compelling vision, ulti-mately solidified his place as a leader who not only spoke the truth but lived it.

The essence of leading with integrity and au-thenticity lies in the alignment of words and actions. Leaders who embody these qualities create a foundation of trust, as their followers can rely on them to act consistently and ethically. This alignment is not only morally sound but also practical; trust is the bedrock of effective leadership. As Stephen Covey, author of *The Speed of Trust*, observes, "Trust is the glue of life. It's the most essential ingredient in effective communication. It's the foundational principle that holds all relationships." Churchill's leadership exemplified this principle, as his transparent communication and steadfast commitment fostered a bond of trust between him and the British people.

Philosophically, the concept of integrity aligns with Aristotle's notion of virtue ethics. Aristotle argued that ethical behavior arises from the cultivation of virtuous character traits, such as honesty, courage, and justice. Integrity, in this context, is not merely about adhering to a set of rules but about embodying virtues that guide one's decisions and interactions. Authenticity complements this framework by emphasizing self-awareness and congruence between one's inner values and outward behavior. Together, integrity and authenticity create a holistic approach to ethical leadership, where actions are grounded in both moral principles and genuine self-expression.

Modern psychology offers further insights into the importance of authenticity in leadership. Research on authentic leadership, pioneered by scholars such as Bruce Avolio and Fred Luthans, highlights four key components: self-aware-ness, relational transparency, balanced process-ing, and internalized moral perspective. These qualities enable leaders to build genuine rela-tionships, make informed decisions, and act in ways that align with their values. Churchill's leadership exemplified these components, as he demonstrated a profound understanding of his strengths and weaknesses, communicated openly with his followers, and remained guided by a moral compass.

Practical applications of leading with integri-ty and authenticity begin with self-reflection. Leaders must cultivate an understanding of their values, motivations, and beliefs to act in alignment with them. For example, a manager striving to lead authentically might reflect on how their personal values influence their decisions and how their actions impact their team. This introspection fosters clarity and consistency, enabling the leader to navigate challenges with confidence and integrity.

Another essential practice is transparent communication. Authentic leaders share information honestly, even when it is difficult or uncomfortable. Churchill's ability to convey both the gravity of Britain's situation and his unwavering resolve inspired confidence and unity. Similarly, modern leaders can build trust by being forthright about challenges while articulating a clear path forward. This transparency not only enhances credibility but also fosters a sense of shared purpose.

Leading with integrity also requires the courage to make principled decisions, even in the face of adversity. Churchill's warnings about Nazi Germany illustrate the importance of standing firm in one's convictions, even when they are unpopular. This principle applies in contemporary contexts as well, where leaders may face pressure to compromise their values for short-term gains. By prioritizing ethical considerations and long-term impact, leaders can navigate these dilemmas with integrity, earning the respect and trust of their followers.

Building authentic relationships is another cornerstone of effective leadership. Authentic leaders prioritize genuine connections, valuing the perspectives and contributions of those they lead. Churchill's rapport with his colleagues and the British public reflected this principle, as he engaged with them not as a distant authority figure but as a fellow citizen invested in their collective success. Modern leaders can cultivate similar relationships by practicing active listening, showing empathy, and fostering collaboration.

Finally, authenticity in leadership requires embracing vulnerability. Leaders who acknowledge their imperfections and share their struggles demonstrate humility and relatability, strengthening their connection with others. Churchill's acknowledgment of the daunting challenges Britain faced, paired with his unshakable optimism, exemplifies this balance. By embracing vulnerability, leaders create an environment where others feel empowered to contribute, take risks, and grow.

As readers reflect on the qualities of integrity and authenticity in leadership, they are encouraged to consider how these principles can be applied in their own lives. What values guide their actions, and how can they ensure that their leadership aligns with these values? By embracing self-awareness, transparent communication, and principled decision-making, individuals can cultivate leadership that not only achieves results but also inspires and uplifts those they lead.

In the words of Winston Churchill, "To each, there comes in their lifetime a special moment when they are figuratively tapped on the shoulder and offered the chance to do a very special thing, unique to their talents. What a tragedy if that moment finds them unprepared or unqualified for that which could have been their finest hour." By leading with integrity and authenticity, individuals can rise to these moments with confidence, creating a legacy of trust, inspiration, and meaningful impact.

Motivating Others Through Shared Vision

At the heart of effective leadership lies the ability to inspire others, not through coercion or authority, but by aligning individuals with a shared vision. A compelling vision has the power to unite people across diverse backgrounds, motivating them to work collaboratively toward a common goal. Great leaders understand that inspiration stems not from the imposition of ideas but from fostering a collective sense of purpose that resonates deeply with each individual. The ability to articulate and embody this vision transforms leaders into catalysts for progress and agents of unity.

One of the most striking examples of leadership through shared vision is the story of Martin Luther King Jr., whose leadership during the American Civil Rights Movement epitomized the transformative power of a unifying goal. King's vision of equality, justice, and harmony was not merely a political ambition but a moral imperative rooted in the ideals of dignity and human rights. His iconic "I Have a Dream" speech painted a vivid picture of a future where all people would be judged by the content of their character rather than the color of their skin.

This vision, grounded in universal values, transcended cultural and geographical boundaries, inspiring millions to join the movement for civil rights.

King's ability to articulate a shared vision was deeply rooted in his understanding of the human experience. He recognized that the struggles of the oppressed were not isolated incidents but reflections of broader injustices. By framing the civil rights struggle as a universal quest for freedom and equality, King connected with people on an emotional and moral level, transforming his vision into a collective aspiration. This approach highlights a fundamental truth about leadership: a shared vision must resonate with the values, hopes, and aspirations of those it seeks to inspire.

Philosophically, the concept of a shared vision aligns with the ideas of existentialism and the quest for meaning. Thinkers like Jean-Paul Sartre and Viktor Frankl emphasized the importance of purpose in navigating life's challenges. For Frankl, who survived the horrors of a concentration camp, the ability to find meaning in suffering was essential for resilience and hope.

Similarly, a shared vision provides individuals with a sense of purpose, enabling them to endure hardships and maintain their commitment to a greater cause. This sense of purpose is not imposed by the leader but emerges organically when the vision aligns with the intrinsic values of the group.

The psychology of motivation also sheds light on the power of shared vision. According to self-determination theory, individuals are most motivated when their actions are aligned with their values, autonomy, and sense of belonging. Leaders who foster a shared vision tap into these intrinsic motivators, creating an environment where individuals feel empowered to contribute their best efforts. For example, during NASA's Apollo program, the vision of landing a man on the moon galvanized engineers, scientists, and astronauts to overcome immense challenges. President John F. Kennedy's declaration, "We choose to go to the moon," framed the mission as a collective endeavor that symbolized human ingenuity and exploration. This shared vision inspired a generation, demonstrating the unifying power of a clear and aspirational goal.

Practical strategies for motivating others through shared vision begin with clarity and communication. A leader must first define the vision with precision, ensuring that it is both inspiring and achievable. Vague or unrealistic visions can lead to confusion and disillusionment, while a well-articulated goal creates a sense of direction and purpose. For instance, a business leader aiming to foster innovation might articulate a vision of creating products that transform lives, connecting employees' efforts to a broader impact on society.

Once the vision is defined, effective communication is essential for fostering alignment. Leaders must not only articulate the vision but also embody it through their actions and decisions. This congruence between words and deeds builds trust and credibility, ensuring that followers perceive the vision as authentic and achievable. Martin Luther King Jr.'s leadership exemplified this principle, as his life and work were consistent with the values of nonviolence, justice, and equality that he espoused.

Collaboration is another cornerstone of motivating others through shared vision. A leader cannot achieve the vision alone; they must inspire and empower others to take ownership of the goal. This involves creating an inclusive environment where every individual feels valued and capable of contributing. Nelson Mandela's leadership during South Africa's transition from apartheid to democracy illustrates the power of collaboration. By fostering dialogue and reconciliation, Mandela united diverse groups under the shared vision of a free and inclusive South Africa. His ability to bring people together, even in the face of deep divisions, demonstrates the transformative potential of collaborative leadership.

Leaders can also motivate others by celebrating progress and reinforcing the vision at every stage of the journey. Milestones and successes, no matter how small, serve as reminders of the collective effort and the importance of the goal. For example, during the civil rights movement, each victory—such as the Montgomery Bus Boycott or the passage of the Civil Rights Act—reinforced the movement's vision and energized its participants. By acknowledging achievements, leaders sustain momentum and inspire continued dedication.

Empathy plays a critical role in fostering alignment with a shared vision. Leaders who understand and address the needs, concerns, and aspirations of their followers build stronger connections and foster loyalty. By actively listening and engaging with their teams, leaders demonstrate that the vision is not solely their own but a collective endeavor shaped by the contributions of every individual. This approach not only strengthens relationships but also enhances the vision's relevance and impact.

As readers reflect on the power of shared vision, they are encouraged to consider their own aspirations and how they align with those they lead. What values and goals inspire them, and how can they communicate these aspirations in a way that resonates with others? By fostering alignment and collaboration, leaders can transform their vision into a collective mission, empowering individuals to achieve extraordinary outcomes together.

In the words of Antoine de Saint-Exupéry, "If you want to build a ship, don't drum up people to collect wood and don't assign them tasks and work, but rather teach them to long for the endless immensity of the sea." This timeless wisdom reminds us that the most effective leaders do not merely direct—they inspire. By motivating others through a shared vision, leaders can create a legacy of unity, progress, and purpose that transcends the boundaries of individual effort.

Creating a Legacy Through Purposeful Leadership

A legacy is the imprint a leader leaves behind, a testament to the vision, values, and impact that defined their leadership. Great leaders do not seek legacy as an end in itself; instead, it becomes the natural outcome of purposeful actions and service to others. Leadership that is rooted in a higher purpose and guided by a commitment to creating positive change transcends individual achievements, inspiring future generations to carry the torch forward.

The concept of legacy is powerfully illustrated in the life of Nelson Mandela. Imprisoned for 27 years due to his fight against apartheid in South Africa, Mandela emerged not embittered but resolute, ready to lead his country toward reconciliation and democracy. His legacy was not simply the dismantling of apartheid but the establishment of a nation founded on principles of unity, equality, and forgiveness. Mandela's willingness to prioritize the well-being of South Africa over personal grievances epitomizes purposeful leadership. His emphasis on healing and inclusivity ensured that his vision extended beyond his lifetime, becoming a guiding framework for South African society.

A leader's legacy is shaped not only by their accomplishments but also by the values they embody and instill in others. Consider the example of Eleanor Roosevelt, whose work as a humanitarian, diplomat, and advocate for human rights left an indelible mark on the world. As the driving force behind the Universal Declaration of Human Rights, Roosevelt demonstrated the enduring power of service-driven leadership. Her ability to champion the dignity and equality of all people, even in the face of resistance, created a legacy that continues to influence international law and human rights movements. Roosevelt's story underscores that a legacy is not defined by the accolades one receives but by the lives one transforms.

Philosophically, the idea of legacy aligns with the Aristotelian concept of *eudaimonia*, or flourishing. Aristotle argued that the highest form of human achievement is to live a life of virtue and purpose, contributing to the greater good. Leadership rooted in this philosophy focuses not on personal gain but on creating lasting value for others. Legacy, in this sense, becomes an extension of a leader's virtuous actions—a ripple effect that perpetuates their influence and ideals.

Creating a legacy through purposeful leadership also requires a long-term perspective. Leaders who focus solely on immediate gains or short-term solutions may achieve momentary success but often fail to create lasting impact. In contrast, those who take a generational view, considering the broader implications of their actions, build foundations that endure. For example, Mahatma Gandhi's philosophy of nonviolence and civil disobedience inspired not only India's independence movement but also subsequent civil rights struggles around the world. Leaders like Martin Luther King Jr. and Nelson Mandela drew from Gandhi's vision, amplifying his legacy across continents and generations.

The process of building a legacy begins with clarity of purpose. Leaders must ask themselves: What do I want to leave behind? How will my actions today shape the world of tomorrow? This self-awareness provides a compass for decision-making, ensuring that each choice aligns with a broader mission. For instance, an entrepreneur committed to environmental sustainability might focus on creating innovative, eco-friendly products, ensuring that their business contributes positively to the planet. By aligning actions with values, leaders can create a legacy that reflects their principles and aspirations.

Service is another cornerstone of legacy-building. Purposeful leaders prioritize the needs of others, recognizing that true influence lies in empowering those they lead. This principle is evident in the life of Fred Rogers, the beloved creator of *Mister Rogers' Neighborhood*. Rogers dedicated his career to educating and nurturing children, emphasizing kindness, empathy, and self-worth. His legacy endures not only in the hearts of those he touched but also in the countless educators and caregivers who continue to embody his values.

Practical strategies for creating a legacy through leadership involve fostering mentorship and succession planning. By investing in the development of others, leaders ensure that their vision and values are carried forward. For example, Steve Jobs's mentorship of Tim Cook and the broader Apple team ensured that the company's culture of innovation and excellence persisted after his passing. This approach reflects an understanding that a leader's influence is magnified through the people they inspire and empower.

Another critical aspect of legacy-building is adaptability. The challenges and opportunities of the present may differ from those of the future, requiring leaders to create frameworks that can evolve over time. Franklin D. Roosevelt's New Deal programs, designed to address the Great Depression, not only stabilized the economy but also established social safety nets that continue to adapt to modern needs. By creating flexible and sustainable systems, leaders ensure that their legacy remains relevant and impactful in a changing world.

Reflection and humility also play essential roles in purposeful leadership. Leaders who regularly evaluate their actions and remain open to feedback demonstrate a commitment to growth and integrity. This self-awareness allows them to refine their approach, ensuring that their efforts align with their mission. For example, Malala Yousafzai, the youngest Nobel laureate, continually reflects on her advocacy for girls' education, adapting her strategies to address emerging challenges. Her humility and dedication have amplified her influence, making her legacy a living, evolving force for change.

As readers reflect on the idea of legacy, they are encouraged to consider their own leadership journey. What values and principles guide their actions? How can they align their efforts with a purpose that transcends personal ambitions? By embracing service, fostering collaboration, and maintaining a long-term perspective, individuals can create a legacy that inspires and uplifts others.

In the words of Maya Angelou, "Your legacy is

every life you have touched." This profound truth reminds us that leadership is not about monuments or accolades but about the enduring impact we have on others. By leading with purpose, integrity, and vision, individuals can create legacies that resonate far beyond their own lifetimes, shaping a brighter and more compassionate world.

CHAPTER 6: THE ROLE OF RELATIONSHIPS – BUILDING CONNECTIONS THAT MATTER

The Power of Meaningful Relationships

Meaningful relationships are among the most potent forces shaping human potential. They provide support, inspiration, and a sense of purpose, acting as catalysts for personal and collective achievements. Throughout history, countless figures have relied on the strength of their relationships to overcome challenges, achieve greatness, and leave enduring legacies. The life of Martin Luther King Jr., a central figure in the American Civil Rights Movement, exemplifies the transformative power of meaningful relationships in advancing a shared vision of equality and justice.

Martin Luther King Jr.'s achievements were not the product of solitary effort but the result of deep, intentional connections with those who shared his ideals and supported his mission. King's relationships with fellow activists, community leaders, and supporters were foundational to the success of the movement. These bonds were built on trust, mutual respect, and a shared commitment to the cause, enabling individuals from diverse backgrounds to unite and work toward a common goal. King's ability to forge and nurture these relationships amplified his influence and strengthened the collective resolve of the movement.

A powerful example of these connections can be found in King's relationship with Reverend Ralph Abernathy, a close friend and collaborator who played a pivotal role in the Civil Rights Movement. Abernathy's unwavering support and leadership complemented King's vision, allowing them to coordinate protests, boycotts, and marches that galvanized the nation. Their partnership exemplified the synergy that arises from meaningful relationships, where mutual trust and a shared purpose create a force greater than the sum of its parts.

The philosophical foundation of meaningful relationships lies in their ability to foster a sense of belonging and shared humanity. Aristotle, in his writings on friendship, described deep relationships as essential for a flourishing life. True friendships, he argued, are based on virtue and mutual goodwill, transcending superficial connections to form bonds that enrich both individuals. King's relationships reflected this

Aristotelian ideal, as they were grounded in a genuine commitment to the well-being of others and a shared pursuit of justice.

Meaningful relationships also play a critical role in resilience, providing emotional support and encouragement during challenging times. King faced immense obstacles, including threats, imprisonment, and the constant pressure of leading a national movement. The strength he derived from his relationships helped him endure these trials and maintain his focus. Coretta Scott King, his wife and steadfast partner, was a source of unwavering support, sharing his vision and providing solace during moments of doubt. Their relationship exemplified the power of mutual understanding and shared purpose in overcoming adversity.

The psychology of meaningful relationships underscores their impact on motivation and achievement. Research in social psychology reveals that individuals are more likely to persevere and succeed when they feel supported by others. This phenomenon, known as the "social facilitation effect," highlights the motivating power of connection. For King, the collective energy of those who marched alongside him and the encouragement of his community reinforced his resolve, propelling him forward even in the face of daunting odds.

The power of meaningful relationships extends beyond personal achievement to create ripple effects that benefit entire communities. King's ability to inspire and mobilize others stemmed from his understanding of the importance of unity and collaboration. He recognized that the movement's strength lay in its collective effort, where individuals supported one another and shared the burden of the struggle. This sense of interconnectedness fostered resilience and solidarity, enabling the movement to achieve milestones such as the Montgomery Bus Boycott, the March on Washington, and the passage of landmark civil rights legislation.

Practical applications of meaningful relationships begin with intentionality. Building deep connections requires time, effort, and a genuine interest in understanding others. Leaders like King demonstrate the importance of listening, empathizing, and valuing diverse perspectives. For instance, King's ability to connect with individuals from different racial, religious, and socioeconomic backgrounds allowed him to build a broad coalition that transcended divisions. Modern readers can apply this principle by seeking out diverse relationships and fostering open, respectful dialogue.

Another essential element of meaningful relationships is vulnerability. Authentic connections are built on trust, which requires individuals to be open about their thoughts, feelings, and challenges. King's willingness to share his fears and struggles with trusted confidants created a sense of authenticity that deepened his relationships. This principle applies to all relationships, whether personal or professional; by embracing vulnerability, individuals can foster trust and create bonds that withstand the test of time.

Collaboration is another cornerstone of meaningful relationships. King's partnerships with organizations such as the Southern Christian Leadership Conference (SCLC) and the Student Nonviolent Coordinating Committee (SNCC) exemplified the power of collective effort. By pooling resources, ideas, and talents, these groups amplified their impact and achieved goals that would have been impossible individually. Modern readers can apply this principle by seeking opportunities for collaboration, recognizing that working together often leads to greater outcomes than working alone.

As readers reflect on the power of meaningful relationships, they are encouraged to consider their own connections and how they shape their lives. Who are the individuals who inspire and support them, and how can they nurture these bonds? By investing in relationships based on trust, empathy, and shared purpose, individuals can create a network of support that enhances their resilience, motivation, and sense of fulfillment.

In the words of Martin Luther King Jr., "Life's most persistent and urgent question is: What are you doing for others?" This profound question underscores the essence of meaningful relationships—their capacity to transform not only the individuals involved but also the broader community. By building connections that matter, individuals can create a foundation for personal growth, collective achievement, and lasting impact.

Cultivating Trust and Empathy in Connections

Trust and empathy are the twin pillars of meaningful and enduring relationships. Together, they create the foundation for connection, understanding, and mutual support. Whether in personal relationships, professional collaborations, or community engagements, these qualities foster a sense of safety and belonging, enabling individuals to work together toward shared goals and navigate challenges with resilience. Cultivating trust and empathy is not a passive process but an intentional practice that strengthens bonds and enriches interactions.

Trust is the cornerstone of any relationship. It allows individuals to feel secure, confident, and valued. Without trust, relationships falter, weighed down by doubt and miscommunication. Building trust requires consistency, reliability, and integrity. The actions and words of trusted individuals align over time, creating a dependable foundation upon which relationships thrive. Consider the bond between Franklin D. Roosevelt and his advisor Harry Hopkins during World War II. Despite Hopkins's failing health, Roosevelt trusted his counsel implicitly, relying on him for critical decisions that shaped the course of the war. Their relationship, grounded in trust, exemplifies how mutual confidence can drive meaningful collaboration and profound impact.

Empathy, on the other hand, is the ability to understand and share the feelings of another. It bridges divides and fosters a sense of shared humanity, enabling individuals to connect on a deeper level. Empathy allows people to see beyond their own perspectives, embracing the experiences and emotions of others. This quality is evident in the leadership of Eleanor Roosevelt, whose empathetic approach to advocacy transformed the way she engaged with the world. As she traveled the globe, visiting troops during wartime and meeting with marginalized communities, Roosevelt demonstrated an unparalleled ability to listen, understand, and act on behalf of those in need. Her empathy not only endeared her to millions but also amplified her influence as a champion of human rights.

The interplay between trust and empathy creates a powerful dynamic. Trust provides the stability needed for relationships to flourish, while empathy deepens understanding and connection. Together, they form the bedrock of collaboration and mutual support. Philosophically, these qualities align with the teachings of Confucius, who emphasized the importance of *ren*—a sense of humanity and compassion—as essential virtues in interpersonal relationships. Confucius believed that by cultivating empathy and trust, individuals could foster harmony within families, communities, and societies.

Modern psychology further underscores the significance of trust and empathy. Research on attachment theory highlights the role of secure relationships in promoting emotional well-being and resilience. Secure attachments, characterized by trust and empathy, provide a safe haven for individuals to explore, grow, and thrive. For example, children who experience consistent care and understanding from their caregivers develop a strong sense of self-worth and confidence, which they carry into adulthood. These principles extend beyond familial bonds, shaping how individuals engage with colleagues, friends, and partners.

Practical strategies for cultivating trust begin with honesty and transparency. Open communication fosters a sense of reliability, allowing individuals to express their thoughts and intentions without fear of judgment. This approach is particularly valuable in professional settings, where trust between team members enhances collaboration and productivity. For instance, during the Apollo space program, NASA engineers and astronauts relied on trust to address complex challenges and innovate solutions. The culture of open communication and mutual respect ensured that every voice was heard, creating a cohesive team capable of extraordinary achievements.

Empathy, too, requires active effort and intentionality. Developing empathy begins with listening—truly listening—to understand another person's perspective. This involves not only hearing their words but also paying attention to nonverbal cues, emotions, and underlying concerns. Empathy also requires setting aside personal biases and judgments, creating space to connect with others on their terms. For example, in conflict resolution, empathetic listening can transform tense situations into opportunities for understanding and compromise. By demonstrating empathy, individuals foster trust and pave the way for deeper, more meaningful connections.

The cultivation of trust and empathy is not without challenges. Misunderstandings, conflicts, and breaches of trust can strain relationships, requiring effort to repair and rebuild. In such moments, humility and accountability become critical. Acknowledging mistakes, offering genuine apologies, and demonstrating a commitment to change are essential steps in restoring trust. Similarly, empathy can be rekindled through acts of kindness and a willingness to reengage with vulnerability and openness.

As readers reflect on their own relationships, they are encouraged to consider how trust and empathy shape their interactions. Are they consistent and reliable in their commitments? Do they listen with an open heart and seek to understand others' perspectives? By embracing these practices, individuals can strengthen their connections and create an environment where trust and empathy flourish.

The benefits of trust and empathy extend far beyond individual relationships. In communities, these qualities foster inclusivity and collaboration, enabling diverse groups to work together toward common goals. In organizations, they enhance morale and innovation, creating a culture of mutual respect and shared purpose. In families, they nurture love and understanding, forming the foundation for lasting bonds.

In the words of Maya Angelou, "I've learned that people will forget what you said, people will forget what you did, but people will never forget how you made them feel." This timeless wisdom captures the essence of trust and empathy—their ability to leave an indelible mark on the hearts and minds of others. By cultivating these qualities, individuals can build connections that not only endure but also inspire, uplift, and transform.

Collaboration as a Catalyst for Success

Collaboration is one of the most potent forces for achieving success, enabling individuals to

combine their strengths, perspectives, and resources to create outcomes far greater than any
could accomplish alone. The history of human
progress is a testament to the power of collaborative efforts, where the pooling of knowledge
and abilities has driven innovation, solved complex challenges, and built enduring legacies.
Collaboration is not simply a practical necessity;
it is a dynamic interplay of trust, shared vision,
and collective effort that amplifies personal and
collective achievements.

One of the most profound examples of collaboration as a catalyst for success is the Apollo space
program, which achieved the monumental goal
of landing humans on the moon in 1969. This
feat was not the result of a single visionary or
even a single team but the culmination of years
of collaborative efforts involving thousands
of engineers, scientists, and astronauts. Under
the leadership of NASA, diverse teams worked
together across disciplines, countries, and cultures to overcome seemingly insurmountable
challenges. The Apollo program illustrates the
immense power of collaboration in turning bold
aspirations into reality. By uniting around a
shared vision, individuals were able to achieve

what once seemed impossible.

Collaboration's transformative potential lies in its ability to harness the diversity of ideas, skills, and experiences. Each person brings unique strengths to the table, and when these are effectively integrated, they create a synergy that enhances creativity and problem-solving. This principle is evident in the lives of innovators like Steve Jobs, whose collaborative leadership at Apple revolutionized industries. Jobs often spoke about the importance of assembling a team of talented individuals who could challenge and complement one another, fostering an environment of creative exchange. The success of groundbreaking products like the iPhone and MacBook stemmed from this collective brilliance, where the contributions of each team member were amplified through collaboration.

Philosophically, the value of collaboration aligns with the concept of interdependence emphasized in many cultural and spiritual traditions. The African philosophy of *Ubuntu*—often summarized as "I am because we are"—captures the essence of human connection and collective effort. This perspective highlights the interconnectedness of individuals and the idea that personal success is deeply linked to the well-being and contributions of others. Collaboration, in this sense, is not just a means to an end but a reflection of the shared humanity that binds us.

Modern psychology reinforces the importance of collaboration in achieving success. Research on group dynamics and team performance reveals that high-functioning teams are characterized by open communication, mutual respect, and a clear understanding of roles and goals. Collaborative environments foster psychological safety, allowing individuals to take risks, share ideas, and learn from mistakes without fear of judgment. This culture of trust and inclusivity enables teams to adapt to challenges and maintain resilience, even in high-pressure situations.

The power of collaboration extends beyond individual achievements to create lasting societal impact. Consider the Civil Rights Movement, where collaborative efforts among leaders, organizations, and communities transformed the social and political landscape of the United States. Figures like Martin Luther King Jr., Rosa Parks, and John Lewis worked in concert with grass-roots activists, churches, and student groups to organize protests, marches, and legal actions. Their collective determination and unity were instrumental in securing landmark legislation such as the Civil Rights Act of 1964 and the Voting Rights Act of 1965. This movement underscores the transformative power of collaboration in addressing systemic challenges and achieving shared goals.

Practical applications of collaboration begin with cultivating a shared vision. Effective collaboration requires a clear and compelling purpose that aligns the efforts of all participants. Leaders play a crucial role in articulating this vision, ensuring that it resonates with the values and aspirations of the team. For example, during the Manhattan Project, which developed the first nuclear weapons, scientists and engineers were united by the goal of ending World War II. While the ethical implications of their work sparked debate, their ability to collaborate effectively under intense pressure and uncertainty demonstrates the power of a shared mission.

Trust and communication are equally vital in

fostering collaboration. Without trust, individuals may hesitate to share ideas or take initiative, undermining the potential for innovation. Open communication ensures that all voices are heard, allowing diverse perspectives to shape decisions and solutions. This principle was evident in the success of the International Space Station (ISS), a collaborative effort involving multiple nations. By prioritizing transparency, cooperation, and mutual respect, participating countries overcame geopolitical differences to build a platform for scientific discovery and exploration.

Another key element of collaboration is adaptability. The ability to adjust strategies and roles in response to changing circumstances enhances the effectiveness of collective efforts. During the Apollo 13 mission, collaboration among NASA's ground team and the astronauts aboard the spacecraft was critical in devising a solution to save the crew after an oxygen tank explosion. Their willingness to adapt, communicate, and pool expertise under extreme pressure exemplifies the resilience of collaborative teams.

As readers reflect on the role of collaboration in

their own lives, they are encouraged to consider how they engage with others to achieve shared goals. Do they actively seek out diverse perspectives and skills? Are they open to feedback and willing to adapt their approach? By embracing these principles, individuals can harness the power of collaboration to amplify their impact and achieve greater success.

In the words of Helen Keller, "Alone we can do so little; together we can do so much." This timeless truth reminds us that collaboration is not just a tool for success but a celebration of human connection and collective potential. By working together with trust, respect, and a shared vision, individuals can overcome challenges, achieve remarkable goals, and create a legacy that endures far beyond their own contributions.

Sustaining and Enriching Lifelong Relationships

Lifelong relationships are among the most rewarding yet complex aspects of the human experience. They provide companionship, support, and a shared history that enriches life in profound ways. However, like all meaningful endeavors, they require care, intention, and effort to thrive. Sustaining and enriching these connections involves a delicate balance of communication, trust, and adaptability, allowing relationships to evolve while maintaining their essence.

At the heart of sustaining lifelong relationships is the principle of consistency. Regular and meaningful interactions keep bonds alive, even across time and distance. This was exemplified in the friendship between John Adams and Thomas Jefferson, two American Founding Fathers who maintained a complex relationship that endured political rivalries and personal differences. Their correspondence, spanning decades, was a testament to their mutual respect and shared commitment to philosophical inquiry. Despite periods of estrangement, they reconciled and enriched their connection through heartfelt letters, demonstrating that consistent effort and open communication can bridge even the widest divides.

The importance of communication in lifelong relationships cannot be overstated. Clear, honest, and empathetic dialogue allows individuals to express their needs, resolve conflicts, and deepen understanding. Philosopher Martin Buber, in his seminal work *I and Thou*, described relationships as sacred encounters that depend on genuine interaction. According to Buber, relationships flourish when individuals engage authentically, recognizing and valuing each other's humanity. This philosophy underscores the transformative power of open communication in nurturing lasting bonds.

Another essential aspect of sustaining relationships is adaptability. Lifelong connections inevitably encounter changes, whether through shifting circumstances, evolving priorities, or personal growth. Embracing these changes with flexibility and understanding ensures that relationships remain relevant and meaningful. Consider the enduring friendship between Maya Angelou and Oprah Winfrey, two influential figures whose lives and careers evolved over decades. Their mutual respect and ability to adapt to each other's changing roles and achievements strengthened their bond, providing a source of inspiration and support for both.

Empathy and forgiveness also play pivotal roles in enriching relationships. No relationship is immune to misunderstandings or conflicts, but the ability to empathize with others' perspectives and offer forgiveness fosters resilience. Nelson Mandela, whose leadership emphasized reconciliation, demonstrated the power of forgiveness in rebuilding fractured relationships. His approach to healing South Africa's divisions serves as a powerful reminder that forgiveness is not about condoning wrongs but about choosing connection over resentment. In personal relationships, this same principle enables individuals to navigate challenges and reaffirm their commitment to one another.

Shared experiences are another cornerstone of lifelong relationships. Engaging in activities that create memories, whether through celebrations, collaborations, or everyday moments, strengthens bonds and provides a foundation for connection. Families, for instance, often find unity through rituals and traditions that reinforce their shared identity. Similarly, friendships that are nurtured through shared adventures, challenges, and joys become deeply rooted, with each experience adding another layer of meaning.

Practically, sustaining relationships also in-volves intentionality in expressing appreciation. Small gestures of gratitude, such as a heartfelt message, a thoughtful gift, or a simple acknowl-edgment of someone's impact, can reinforce bonds and remind others of their value. Con-sider the example of Fred Rogers, who main-tained lifelong friendships through his genuine kindness and habit of writing letters to those he cared about. His practice of intentional appre-ciation left a lasting impression on countless individuals, illustrating the profound effect of even small acts of gratitude.

Another practical strategy is the cultivation of patience. Lifelong relationships are not immune to moments of frustration or impatience, but the willingness to endure these moments with grace preserves their longevity. This patience often involves setting aside ego, choosing to prioritize the relationship over being right. For example, in professional partnerships like the Wright brothers, whose collaboration revolutionized aviation, patience and mutual respect allowed them to navigate disagreements and maintain their shared vision.

Investing in personal growth is also essential for sustaining relationships. When individuals commit to their own development, they bring renewed energy, perspective, and strength to their connections. This growth fosters mutual inspiration, as each person's evolution enriches the relationship. For instance, the lifelong marriage of Ruth and Martin Ginsburg thrived on their shared commitment to personal and professional growth. Ruth's rise as a Supreme Court Justice and Martin's success as a tax law expert were celebrated and supported by each other, demonstrating the symbiotic nature of growth in relationships.

In reflecting on lifelong relationships, it is important to consider how one's own actions contribute to their health and vitality. Are there moments when more effort could be made to connect, listen, or show appreciation? Are there opportunities to practice forgiveness, empathy, or patience? By embracing these qualities, individuals can sustain and enrich their connections, creating bonds that withstand the test of time.

Lifelong relationships are not static; they are living, evolving entities that require care and attention. As readers reflect on the relationships in their lives, they are encouraged to approach them with intention and gratitude. By nurturing these connections, they can create a network of support and joy that enriches every aspect of life.

In the words of poet Rainer Maria Rilke, "A person isn't who they are during the last conversation you had with them—they're who they've been throughout your whole relationship." This sentiment reminds us that relationships are defined not by singular moments but by the ongoing effort, love, and commitment invested over time. By embracing these principles, individuals can create relationships that not only endure but also flourish, becoming a source of strength, meaning, and fulfillment.

CHAPTER 7: THE LEGACY MINDSET – CREATING MEANING BEYOND THE SELF

Defining Legacy and Its Role in Fulfillment

Legacy is the enduring mark we leave on the world, a reflection of our values, actions, and the impact we have on others. It is the thread that connects the transient moments of our lives to something greater—a narrative that outlives us, shaping the lives of those who follow. Living a legacy-driven life transcends the pursuit of personal success, offering a sense of purpose and fulfillment that arises from knowing one's contributions have meaning beyond the self.

The concept of legacy is not limited to monumental achievements or public accolades. It is found in the relationships we nurture, the values we impart, and the ways in which we touch the lives of others. A legacy-driven life is one lived with intention, where each decision is guided by the question: What impact will this have on the future? This perspective shifts the focus from immediate gratification to lasting significance, encouraging individuals to consider how their actions align with their aspirations for the world they wish to create.

One of the most enduring examples of a legacy-driven life is the story of Mahatma Gandhi, whose commitment to nonviolence and justice transformed not only India but also the global fight for human rights. Gandhi's legacy was not simply the political independence of India but the philosophy of *Satyagraha* — the force of truth and nonviolent resistance — that continues to inspire movements for social change worldwide. His life illustrates the power of aligning one's actions with a higher purpose, creating a legacy that transcends time and geography. Gandhi's legacy reminds us that a meaningful life is not measured by the accolades one receives but by the lives one uplifts.

The philosophical foundation of legacy lies in the human desire for meaning. Thinkers like Viktor Frankl, author of *Man's Search for Meaning*, emphasized the importance of purpose in navigating life's challenges. According to Frankl, meaning is found not in what we take from the world but in what we give to it. Legacy, in this sense, is the culmination of a life lived with purpose — a testament to the values and contributions that define our existence. This perspective shifts the narrative of fulfillment from individual achievements to collective impact, encouraging individuals to seek meaning through service and connection.

Modern psychology echoes this understanding, highlighting the role of legacy in fostering well-being and fulfillment. Research on generativity, a concept introduced by psychologist Erik Erikson, reveals that individuals who focus on contributing to future generations experience greater life satisfaction and emotional resilience. Generativity involves actions that nurture, mentor, or inspire others, creating a sense of continuity and purpose. For example, a teacher who dedicates their career to educating and empowering students may find profound fulfillment in knowing their efforts shape the lives of countless individuals. This sense of generativity is a hallmark of a legacy-driven life.

Living with a legacy mindset does not require grand gestures or public recognition. It begins with small, intentional actions that align with one's values and aspirations. Consider the example of Fred Rogers, the creator of *Mister Rogers' Neighborhood*. Through his television program, Rogers conveyed messages of kindness, empathy, and acceptance, leaving an indelible mark on generations of children. His legacy was not built on fame or fortune but on his unwavering commitment to nurturing the emotional well-being of others. Rogers's life illustrates that a legacy-driven mindset is accessible to anyone who approaches their actions with intention and care.

Practical steps toward a legacy-driven life begin with self-reflection. Individuals must ask themselves: What values do I want to embody? What impact do I hope to have on others? By clarifying these intentions, individuals can align their actions with their aspirations, creating a cohesive narrative of purpose and contribution. For example, someone who values environmental sustainability might focus on reducing their carbon footprint, educating others about climate change, or supporting organizations dedicated to conservation. These actions, though seemingly small, contribute to a larger legacy of environmental stewardship.

Another essential aspect of living a legacy-driven life is cultivating relationships. Legacy is not created in isolation; it is shaped through interactions with others. By nurturing connections based on trust, empathy, and shared purpose, individuals create a network of influence that amplifies their impact. A mentor who invests in the growth and development of their mentees, for instance, leaves a legacy not only in the lives of those they guide but also in the ripple effects of their mentees' achievements. This interconnectedness highlights the relational nature of legacy and its role in fostering fulfillment.

Resilience and adaptability are also critical to building a legacy. Life is filled with uncertainties and challenges, but a legacy-driven mindset provides a compass for navigating these obstacles. Consider the story of Helen Keller, whose determination to overcome the limitations of blindness and deafness allowed her to become a writer, activist, and advocate for social justice. Keller's legacy was shaped not by her circumstances but by her unwavering commitment to making a difference. Her life illustrates that resilience, guided by purpose, transforms adversity into opportunity.

As readers reflect on the concept of legacy, they are encouraged to consider how their own actions contribute to the world around them. What values do they hope to pass on? How can their daily choices reflect their aspirations for the future? By embracing these questions, individuals can cultivate a legacy mindset that enriches their lives and inspires those they touch.

In the words of Maya Angelou, "Your legacy is every life you have touched." This profound truth reminds us that legacy is not about monuments or accolades but about the enduring impact of our actions, words, and relationships. By living with purpose and intention, individuals can create a legacy that transcends their lifetime, leaving the world a better place for future generations.

Learning from Philanthropy and Service

Philanthropy and service are among the most profound ways individuals can create a lasting impact. Through acts of generosity and dedication, individuals not only address immediate needs but also lay the groundwork for enduring change. The legacies of figures like Mother Teresa and Andrew Carnegie illustrate the transformative power of service, demonstrating how selflessness and vision can uplift entire communities and inspire future generations.

Mother Teresa's life is a testament to the impact of service rooted in compassion and humility. Born Anjezë Gonxhe Bojaxhiu in 1910, she dedicated her life to serving the poorest of the poor, founding the Missionaries of Charity in 1950. Her work in the slums of Kolkata (formerly Calcutta) focused on providing care for the sick, the destitute, and the dying—those often overlooked by society. For Mother Teresa, service was not about grand gestures or material wealth but about offering dignity and love to every individual she encountered.

The legacy of Mother Teresa lies not only in the tangible impact of her work but also in the values she embodied: kindness, empathy, and unwavering commitment to others. She once said, "Not all of us can do great things. But we can do small things with great love." This perspective underscores the idea that service is accessible to everyone, regardless of their resources or circumstances. By approaching each act of kindness with intention and compassion, individuals contribute to a legacy of care that ripples outward, touching countless lives.

In contrast, Andrew Carnegie's approach to philanthropy was shaped by his immense wealth and a strategic vision for societal improvement. As one of the wealthiest individuals of his time, Carnegie amassed a fortune through his leadership in the steel industry. However, he believed that wealth came with a moral obligation to benefit society—a principle he articulated in his essay, *The Gospel of Wealth*. Carnegie argued that the wealthy should act as stewards of their fortunes, using their resources to address social issues and promote the public good.

Carnegie's philanthropy focused on creating opportunities for education and self-improvement. He funded the construction of over 2,500 libraries worldwide, believing that access to knowledge was a cornerstone of personal and societal progress. He also established institutions such as Carnegie Mellon University and the Carnegie Foundation, which continue to advance education, science, and culture. Carnegie's legacy demonstrates the power of strategic philanthropy in creating systems and structures that enable others to thrive long after the bene-factor is gone.

The lives of Mother Teresa and Andrew Car-negie reflect two distinct but complementary approaches to service. While Mother Teresa's work emphasized direct, personal engagement, Carnegie's philanthropy focused on systemic change. Both approaches highlight the trans-formative potential of service, whether through individual acts of kindness or large-scale initia-tives. Together, they illustrate that the path to leaving a legacy through service is as diverse as the individuals who undertake it.

Philosophically, the concept of service aligns with the idea of altruism—the selfless concern for the well-being of others. Altruism has been explored in various traditions, from the teach-ings of Jesus and Buddha to the writings of modern philosophers like Peter Singer. Sing-er's concept of "effective altruism" emphasizes using resources in ways that yield the greatest benefit, echoing Carnegie's strategic approach to philanthropy. Meanwhile, Mother Teresa's work reflects a more personal, spiritual under-standing of service, rooted in the belief that every act of care has intrinsic value.

The psychological benefits of service further underscore its significance in creating lasting impact. Research shows that acts of kindness and generosity enhance emotional well-being, fostering a sense of connection and purpose. This phenomenon, often referred to as the "helper's high," highlights the reciprocal nature of service: while benefiting others, individuals also enrich their own lives. For example, volunteers who dedicate time to mentoring, teaching, or community work often report increased happiness and fulfillment, driven by the knowledge that their efforts make a difference.

Practical applications of philanthropy and service begin with identifying areas of passion and need. Individuals can ask themselves: What causes resonate with me? Where can I make the most meaningful contribution? Whether it's supporting education, healthcare, environmental conservation, or social justice, aligning one's efforts with personal values ensures that acts of service are both impactful and fulfilling. For example, a business leader passionate about sustainability might focus on reducing their company's environmental footprint, while a teacher might dedicate time to mentoring underserved students.

Another important aspect of meaningful service is collaboration. Working with others amplifies impact, allowing individuals to pool resources, ideas, and expertise. The success of organizations like Habitat for Humanity, which relies on volunteer efforts to build homes for those in need, demonstrates the power of collective action. By joining forces with like-minded individuals or organizations, individuals can contribute to initiatives that create lasting change.

Service also requires a long-term perspective. While immediate acts of kindness are valuable, creating a legacy through service often involves sustained effort and commitment. For instance, Carnegie's decision to fund libraries was not a one-time gesture but a lifelong dedication to empowering communities. Similarly, modern philanthropists like Melinda French Gates have demonstrated the importance of persistence in addressing complex issues such as global health and gender equality. These examples underscore that meaningful service is not about short-term results but about building a foundation for enduring progress.

As readers reflect on the role of service in their own lives, they are encouraged to consider how their actions align with their aspirations for the world. What causes inspire them, and how can they contribute to those causes in ways that reflect their values and resources? By embracing a mindset of service, individuals can create a legacy that extends far beyond their own achievements, shaping a better future for generations to come.

In the words of Albert Schweitzer, "The purpose of human life is to serve, and to show compassion and the will to help others." This sentiment captures the essence of service as a path to fulfillment and legacy. By dedicating time, energy, and resources to the well-being of others, individuals can create a legacy of generosity and compassion that resonates across time and space.

Crafting a Vision for Future Generations

Legacy is not merely an accumulation of actions but the deliberate shaping of a vision that endures. To craft a meaningful legacy, individuals must consider how their values and ambitions align with the future they wish to create. It is an intentional process that calls for reflection, imagination, and a commitment to contributing to the world in ways that resonate deeply with personal principles. By envisioning a legacy that reflects one's unique perspective, individuals can inspire and empower future generations, ensuring that their contributions transcend the limits of their own time.

A compelling example of crafting a legacy vision is found in the life of Nelson Mandela. After spending 27 years in prison for his anti-apartheid activism, Mandela emerged not with a focus on retribution but on reconciliation. His vision was clear: a South Africa united by equality, justice, and forgiveness. This vision was not only rooted in Mandela's personal experiences and values but also aimed at fostering a harmonious and inclusive society for generations to come. His ability to articulate and embody this vision transformed him into a symbol of hope and resilience, inspiring others to continue his work long after his leadership ended.

Mandela's approach illustrates an essential aspect of legacy: alignment with personal values. A legacy built on authenticity and integrity resonates far more deeply than one based on external expectations or fleeting ambitions. Individuals who align their actions with their core beliefs create a sense of coherence and purpose that inspires trust and admiration. For example, an entrepreneur who prioritizes sustainability because they genuinely value environmental stewardship is more likely to leave a lasting impact than someone who adopts sustainability as a trend. Authenticity ensures that the legacy is not only meaningful to the individual but also relatable and enduring for others.

Philosophically, the act of crafting a legacy aligns with the idea of stewardship—the responsibility to nurture and protect what has been entrusted to us for the benefit of future generations. Indigenous cultures around the world often emphasize the principle of considering the "seventh generation," ensuring that decisions made today honor the well-being of those who will live centuries from now. This perspective shifts the focus from immediate gains to long-term impact, encouraging individuals to think expansively about the ripple effects of their actions.

To craft a vision for future generations, reflection is a vital first step. This process begins with asking profound questions: What values define me? What causes ignite my passion? How do I want to be remembered, and what impact do I hope to have? By engaging in this introspection, individuals can identify the principles and ambitions that will guide their legacy. For example, a teacher may recognize a deep commitment to empowering students through education, shaping a vision that emphasizes access to learning opportunities for underserved communities.

Historical figures provide rich insights into how personal values and ambitions can shape a legacy. Consider the life of Jane Addams, the founder of Hull House and a pioneer in social work. Addams's vision was rooted in her commitment to social justice and community welfare. Her efforts to provide housing, education, and resources for immigrants and low-income families in Chicago not only addressed immediate needs but also laid the foundation for the modern social work profession. Addams's legacy demonstrates how aligning one's actions with a vision can create lasting structures that continue to benefit society long after the individual's lifetime.

Another key element in crafting a legacy vision is imagination—the ability to envision possibilities beyond current limitations. This requires thinking creatively about how one's contributions can evolve and adapt over time. For example, Andrew Carnegie's vision of public libraries as centers for self-improvement and education extended beyond his own era, as the institutions he established continue to empower individuals worldwide. Imagination allows individuals to design legacies that are not only impactful in the present but also adaptable to future needs and contexts.

Collaboration also plays a significant role in shaping a legacy vision. No individual legacy exists in isolation; it is influenced by and contributes to a larger tapestry of collective effort. For instance, the environmental legacy of Rachel Carson, author of *Silent Spring*, was amplified by the work of activists, scientists, and policy-makers who carried her message forward. Her vision of environmental stewardship became a rallying cry for the modern environmental movement, illustrating how collaboration can transform a personal legacy into a global phenomenon.

Practical strategies for crafting a legacy vision involve setting clear, actionable goals that align with one's values and aspirations. For instance, a philanthropist dedicated to advancing healthcare might establish a foundation focused on medical research, ensuring that their resources are directed toward long-term solutions. Similarly, an artist might create works that provoke thought and inspire change, leaving behind a cultural legacy that continues to resonate.

Flexibility and adaptability are also crucial in legacy-building. The world is constantly changing, and a rigid vision risks becoming obsolete. Individuals must be willing to revisit and refine their vision as circumstances evolve. For example, tech innovators like Elon Musk continuously adapt their projects and goals to align with emerging opportunities and challenges, ensuring their legacies remain relevant and impactful.

As readers consider how to craft their own vision for future generations, they are encouraged to embrace both introspection and action. What values and causes matter most to them? How can they translate these ideals into tangible contributions? By engaging with these questions, individuals can begin to shape a legacy that reflects their deepest aspirations and creates meaningful change.

In the words of John Quincy Adams, "If your actions inspire others to dream more, learn more, do more, and become more, you are a leader." This timeless wisdom underscores the essence of a legacy mindset: the ability to inspire and empower others through values-driven actions. By crafting a vision that aligns with their principles, individuals can create a legacy that not only honors their own journey but also enriches the lives of future generations.

Taking Action to Build Your Legacy Today

A legacy is not something reserved for the end

of life or a distant future—it is shaped in the choices and actions we take every day. The concept of legacy is both empowering and practical, as it reminds us that our lives have the potential to leave a lasting impact. By embracing intentionality and purpose, individuals can begin crafting a meaningful legacy at any stage of life, regardless of their resources, circumstances, or career paths.

The first step in building a legacy is recognizing that small, consistent actions often have the greatest impact over time. This idea is powerfully illustrated in the life of Fred Rogers, who created *Mister Rogers' Neighborhood*. Rogers's legacy was not defined by grand gestures but by his daily commitment to nurturing kindness, empathy, and emotional well-being in children. Every episode he produced reflected his values, creating a ripple effect that has influenced generations. Rogers's story highlights the importance of aligning everyday actions with one's values and aspirations, demonstrating that legacy-building begins in the present moment.

Living with intention requires clarity of purpose. Taking time to reflect on personal values and goals is essential for aligning actions with the legacy one wishes to create. This process might involve journaling, seeking guidance from mentors, or simply asking profound questions: What do I stand for? What impact do I want to have on the people around me? By exploring these questions, individuals can identify the principles that will guide their choices. For instance, someone passionate about education may decide to volunteer as a tutor, sponsor scholarships, or advocate for policy changes in their community. These actions, while seemingly modest, contribute to a broader legacy of empowerment and learning.

Building a legacy also requires courage—the willingness to act even in the face of uncertainty or doubt. Historical figures like Rosa Parks exemplify this principle. Her decision to remain seated on a segregated bus in Montgomery, Alabama, sparked a movement that changed the course of American history. Parks did not set out to create a legacy that day; she simply acted in alignment with her values of justice and equality. Her courage reminds us that legacy-building is not about seeking recognition but about standing firm in one's convictions.

Similarly, individuals today can take meaningful steps toward their goals, knowing that even
small acts of bravery can lead to transformative
change.

Collaboration is another essential component
of building a legacy. Few legacies are created in
isolation; they are often the result of collective
effort and shared vision. Consider the example of Habitat for Humanity, an organization
built on the principle of communities coming
together to provide housing for those in need.
Founded by Millard and Linda Fuller, Habitat
for Humanity demonstrates how collaboration
amplifies impact. By working with others who
share similar values and goals, individuals can
achieve results that extend far beyond their personal reach.

Mentorship is one of the most direct and powerful ways to begin creating a legacy. By investing
time and energy in the growth of others, individuals ensure that their values and knowledge
are carried forward. A teacher who inspires
students to pursue their passions, a coach who
instills resilience and discipline in their team, or
a business leader who nurtures the potential of

their employees—all of these acts of mentorship contribute to a lasting legacy. These relationships often have ripple effects, as those who are mentored go on to inspire and mentor others, creating a chain of positive influence that spans generations.

Adaptability is also crucial for legacy-building. Life is unpredictable, and the path to achieving one's goals is rarely linear. The ability to reassess and adjust one's approach ensures that efforts remain relevant and effective. This principle is evident in the life of Eleanor Roosevelt, who adapted her roles and contributions throughout her lifetime. From serving as First Lady to championing human rights as a United Nations delegate, Roosevelt continually reinvented her legacy to meet the needs of the times. Her adaptability serves as a reminder that legacy-building is a dynamic process, shaped by changing circumstances and opportunities.

To take action today, individuals must also recognize the power of generosity. Generosity is not limited to financial contributions; it includes time, energy, and expertise. Andrew Carnegie, whose philanthropic legacy includes the establishment of libraries and educational institutions, believed that wealth should be used for the greater good. Yet generosity is equally impactful on a smaller scale — whether it's volunteering at a local shelter, mentoring a colleague, or simply offering support to a friend in need. These acts of giving, no matter how modest, contribute to a legacy of compassion and care.

Practical tools for building a legacy include setting specific, actionable goals. These goals might be personal, such as committing to daily acts of kindness, or professional, such as leading a project that aligns with one's values. By breaking these goals into manageable steps, individuals can create a roadmap for their legacy-building journey. For instance, someone passionate about environmental conservation might start by reducing their carbon footprint, organizing community cleanups, or advocating for policy changes. Each step, though small, contributes to a larger narrative of impact.

Finally, gratitude and reflection play an integral role in legacy-building. Taking time to acknowledge the progress made and the relationships that have shaped one's journey fosters a sense of fulfillment and purpose. Regularly reflecting on how one's actions align with their values ensures that efforts remain intentional and meaningful. In the words of Maya Angelou, "Be a rainbow in someone's cloud." This sentiment captures the essence of legacy-building: small acts of kindness and care create ripples that brighten the lives of others, leaving a lasting impact.

As readers consider how to take action in building their own legacies, they are encouraged to start with the present moment. What choices can they make today that align with their values? How can they contribute to the lives of others, no matter how modest the effort? By embracing intentionality, collaboration, and generosity, individuals can create legacies that reflect their highest aspirations and inspire those around them.

Legacy is not an abstract concept or a distant goal—it is the culmination of the choices and actions we take each day. By living with purpose and courage, individuals can begin building a legacy that transcends their lifetime, leaving the world a richer and more compassionate place.

CHAPTER 8: THE FULFILLMENT PARADOX – REDEFINING SUCCESS

Challenging Conventional Success Metrics

For centuries, the pursuit of success has been tethered to external markers: wealth, status, power, and accolades. These metrics, deeply ingrained in societal norms, often dictate aspirations and shape how individuals measure their achievements. Yet history and philosophy reveal a profound truth—success, as conventionally defined, often falls short of delivering fulfillment. Figures like Viktor Frankl, who redefined success through the lens of purpose and meaning, challenge us to reconsider what it truly means to lead a successful life.

Viktor Frankl's life and work exemplify the power of purpose in redefining success. As a Holocaust survivor and author of *Man's Search for Meaning*, Frankl endured unimaginable suffering in Nazi concentration camps. Stripped of all external markers of success—possessions, status, freedom, and even family—Frankl was left with one resource: his inner world. In the face of despair, he discovered that meaning, not material wealth or status, was the cornerstone of human resilience and fulfillment. His belief that "those who have a 'why' to live can bear with almost any 'how'" underscores the transformative potential of purpose in reshaping the concept of success.

Frankl's insights challenge the conventional narrative that equates success with accumulation and achievement. Instead, he posits that true success lies in the ability to find meaning in life's experiences, even in adversity. His life serves as a powerful reminder that external circumstances do not define our worth; rather, it is the values we uphold and the contributions we make that leave a lasting impact. Frankl's perspective invites individuals to move beyond the superficial and embrace a deeper, more authentic understanding of success.

The philosophical roots of this redefinition can be traced to ancient wisdom. Stoic philosophers like Epictetus emphasized the importance of focusing on what is within one's control—attitudes, choices, and virtues—rather than external outcomes. For the Stoics, success was not a matter of public recognition or material gain but of living a virtuous and meaningful life. This perspective aligns with Frankl's emphasis on purpose, as both philosophies prioritize internal alignment over external validation.

Modern psychology reinforces the importance of purpose as a foundation for fulfillment. Studies on well-being consistently show that individuals who connect their actions to a sense of purpose experience greater life satisfaction, resilience, and happiness. For example, researchers have found that people who engage in work they find meaningful are not only more motivated but also better equipped to navigate challenges. This shift in focus—from external rewards to intrinsic values—reshapes the narrative of success, placing fulfillment at the center.

Challenging conventional success metrics requires courage and introspection. It involves questioning societal expectations and resisting the pressure to conform to traditional definitions of achievement. This process is not without its difficulties, as it often involves unlearning deeply ingrained beliefs. Yet history provides numerous examples of individuals who embraced this challenge, forging paths that prioritized purpose over prestige.

Consider the life of Mahatma Gandhi, who left behind a promising legal career in South Africa to dedicate himself to the pursuit of justice and nonviolence. Gandhi's decision to align his life with his values, despite the sacrifices it entailed, redefined success on his own terms. His legacy, rooted in service and resilience, demonstrates that purpose-driven lives often leave the most profound and enduring marks on the world.

Similarly, the story of Jane Goodall, renowned primatologist and conservationist, illustrates how redefining success can lead to extraordinary contributions. Goodall's decision to study chimpanzees in their natural habitat defied conventional academic paths and expectations for women in science during her time. Yet her work, driven by a deep sense of purpose, transformed our understanding of primates and reshaped the global conversation on conservation. Goodall's journey exemplifies the fulfillment that arises from pursuing a mission aligned with one's values, even in the face of societal skepticism.

Redefining success also involves shifting the focus from individual gain to collective impact. Purpose often extends beyond personal fulfillment to include contributions that uplift others and benefit communities. This perspective resonates with the concept of *eudaimonia*—the ancient Greek idea of flourishing through virtuous living. Aristotle argued that true success is achieved by living in harmony with one's values and contributing to the greater good. This timeless wisdom encourages individuals to view success not as a solitary pursuit but as a shared endeavor that enhances both personal and collective well-being.

Practical steps toward challenging conventional success metrics begin with self-reflection. Individuals are encouraged to ask themselves: What truly matters to me? What kind of impact do I want to have? By clarifying these intentions, they can align their actions with their unique definitions of success. This alignment often involves letting go of societal expectations and embracing a more personal and meaningful approach to achievement.

Another important aspect of this redefinition is cultivating resilience in the face of judgment or doubt. Choosing to prioritize purpose over conventional markers of success may invite criticism or misunderstanding, yet it is through this resilience that individuals find strength and authenticity. For example, artists who create work that reflects their inner truths, rather than catering to popular trends, often leave the most lasting and impactful legacies.

As readers consider how to redefine success in their own lives, they are encouraged to reflect on the values, passions, and aspirations that bring them meaning. What would success look like if stripped of societal expectations? How might they align their daily choices with this deeper understanding? By embracing these questions, individuals can begin to craft a narrative of success that resonates with their authentic selves.

In the words of Ralph Waldo Emerson, "To laugh often and much; to win the respect of intelligent people and the affection of children; to earn the appreciation of honest critics and endure the betrayal of false friends; to appreciate beauty; to find the best in others; to leave the world a bit better... This is to have succeeded." Emerson's reflection reminds us that success is not confined to wealth or status but is found in the values we embody, the lives we touch, and the purpose we pursue. By challenging conventional metrics and embracing a legacy of meaning, individuals can redefine success on their own terms, creating a life that is both fulfilling and impactful.

The Connection Between Purpose and Fulfillment

Purpose is the invisible thread that ties our actions to a greater sense of meaning, transforming the ordinary into the extraordinary. It provides direction, fuels motivation, and shapes the contours of a fulfilling life. When individuals align their actions with a clear sense of purpose, they experience a profound shift: the pursuit of goals becomes deeply satisfying, and even challenges become opportunities for growth. The connection between purpose and fulfillment is not merely theoretical—it is a lived reality demonstrated by history's most impactful figures and supported by timeless philosophical insights.

Consider the life of Albert Schweitzer, a theologian, physician, and Nobel Peace Prize laureate. Schweitzer's sense of purpose was rooted in his philosophy of *reverence for life*, which emphasized the intrinsic value of all living beings. This belief guided his decision to leave a comfortable academic career in Europe and dedicate his life to providing medical care in Africa. Despite the hardships he faced, Schweitzer's alignment with his purpose gave him an enduring sense of fulfillment. He once said, "The only ones among you who will be really happy are those who will have sought and found how to serve." His life illustrates how purpose-driven actions elevate personal satisfaction by connecting individual efforts to a broader, meaningful impact.

The connection between purpose and fulfillment is also explored in Viktor Frankl's seminal work, *Man's Search for Meaning*. Drawing on his experiences in Nazi concentration camps, Frankl observed that individuals who found a sense of purpose, even in the most harrowing conditions, were more resilient and fulfilled than those who lacked direction. For Frankl, purpose was not tied to circumstances but to the ability to find meaning in one's existence. He described this as a form of self-transcendence—a state where individuals move beyond their own needs and desires to contribute to something greater. This philosophy resonates with the idea that purpose bridges the gap between personal fulfillment and collective impact, creating a ripple effect of meaning.

From a psychological perspective, the alignment of actions with purpose is a key driver of well-being. Positive psychology, a field pioneered by Martin Seligman, highlights the concept of *eudaimonic happiness*—a deep sense of contentment derived from living in accordance with one's values and aspirations. Unlike fleeting pleasure, eudaimonic happiness is rooted in purpose and engagement, offering a sustainable source of fulfillment. Studies have shown that individuals who feel connected to a sense of purpose are more likely to experience greater resilience, better health, and stronger relationships. This research underscores the transformative power of aligning actions with purpose, not just for individual well-being but for the broader community.

The practical implications of aligning actions with purpose are far-reaching. It begins with self-awareness—understanding one's values, passions, and aspirations. Purpose is not something external to be discovered but an internal compass to be cultivated. This process often involves introspection and experimentation, as individuals explore what brings them joy, meaning, and a sense of contribution. For example, a young activist passionate about environmental sustainability might find fulfillment in organizing community cleanups, advocating for policy changes, or educating others about climate change. By aligning their actions with their purpose, they not only achieve personal satisfaction but also contribute to a cause that extends beyond themselves.

The importance of purpose is further highlighted in the realm of leadership. Purpose-driven leaders, such as Nelson Mandela and Malala Yousafzai, have demonstrated that aligning their actions with a clear mission inspires others and fosters collective progress. Mandela's unwavering commitment to justice and reconciliation guided his leadership in dismantling apartheid and building a more equitable South Africa. Similarly, Yousafzai's advocacy for girls' education, rooted in her personal experiences and values, has sparked a global movement for educational equity. These examples show that purpose is not only a source of personal fulfillment but also a catalyst for societal transformation.

Philosophically, the connection between purpose and fulfillment aligns with the teachings of Aristotle, who described a meaningful life as one driven by *telos*, or an ultimate goal. Aristotle argued that fulfillment arises from living in accordance with one's *arete*, or excellence, and contributing to the common good. This ancient wisdom remains relevant today, reminding individuals that purpose is both a personal and collective endeavor.

While purpose provides direction, its fulfillment often requires perseverance and adaptability. Life is unpredictable, and circumstances may challenge the pursuit of one's goals. Yet it is in these moments of adversity that the strength of purpose becomes most evident. Consider the life of Helen Keller, who overcame the challenges of blindness and deafness to become an advocate for disability rights and education. Her purpose-driven actions, despite formidable obstacles, brought fulfillment not only to her own life but also to countless others who benefited from her advocacy. Keller's story exemplifies the resilience that purpose fosters, enabling in-

dividuals to navigate setbacks while remaining
anchored to their values.

The connection between purpose and fulfillment
is also evident in small, everyday actions. Acts
of kindness, generosity, and creativity, when
aligned with one's values, contribute to a sense
of meaning and satisfaction. A parent who takes
time to nurture their child's curiosity, a teacher
who inspires students to pursue their dreams, or
an artist who channels their passion into their
work—all are examples of purpose in action.
These moments, though seemingly ordinary,
create a foundation for fulfillment by aligning
daily efforts with a larger sense of meaning.

As readers reflect on their own lives, they are
encouraged to explore how their actions align
with their purpose. Are they dedicating time to
what truly matters to them? Are their choices
guided by their values and aspirations? By engaging with these questions, individuals can
begin to cultivate a deeper connection between
their actions and their sense of fulfillment.

In the words of Howard Thurman, "Don't ask
what the world needs. Ask what makes you

come alive, and go do it. Because what the world needs is people who have come alive." This profound wisdom captures the essence of the connection between purpose and fulfillment: by aligning actions with what makes us come alive, we not only enrich our own lives but also contribute to the well-being of others. Purpose is the bridge that transforms effort into meaning, creating a life that is both deeply satisfying and profoundly impactful.

The Role of Gratitude in Achieving Fulfillment

Gratitude is a powerful force that transforms how we experience the world. It shifts focus from what is lacking to what is abundant, fostering a sense of contentment and connection that transcends material circumstances. When integrated into daily life, gratitude becomes more than an emotional response—it becomes a guiding principle that enhances joy and fulfillment. By embracing gratitude, individuals unlock a deeper appreciation for life's blessings, finding meaning in the ordinary and extraordinary alike.

The transformative potential of gratitude is evident in the life and teachings of Maya Angelou. Angelou, an acclaimed poet, author, and civil rights activist, faced significant challenges throughout her life, including poverty, discrimination, and personal trauma. Yet she consistently emphasized the importance of gratitude as a source of strength and resilience. In her autobiography, Angelou wrote, "This is a wonderful day. I've never seen this one before." Her ability to approach each day with curiosity and appreciation exemplifies the profound impact of a gratitude-driven mindset. For Angelou, gratitude was not a denial of life's difficulties but a recognition of its inherent beauty and potential.

Philosophically, gratitude has been explored as a cornerstone of well-being across cultures and traditions. In ancient Stoicism, for example, gratitude was considered essential for cultivating inner peace. Marcus Aurelius, the Roman emperor and Stoic philosopher, frequently reflected on his blessings in his *Meditations*. By acknowledging the kindness of others and the gifts of nature, Aurelius grounded himself in a sense of interconnectedness and purpose. This practice of gratitude allowed him to navigate the pressures of leadership and adversity with grace, demonstrating its relevance even in the most challenging circumstances.

Modern psychology echoes these insights, revealing the profound benefits of gratitude on mental health and fulfillment. Research has shown that individuals who practice gratitude experience increased happiness, reduced stress, and improved relationships. One study conducted by psychologists Robert Emmons and Michael McCullough found that participants who kept a gratitude journal reported greater life satisfaction and optimism than those who focused on neutral or negative aspects of their lives. This evidence underscores the transformative power of gratitude as a tool for enhancing emotional well-being and fostering a positive outlook.

The role of gratitude in fulfillment extends beyond personal benefits; it also strengthens connections with others. Expressing gratitude deepens relationships by acknowledging the contributions and kindness of those around us. This dynamic creates a cycle of mutual appreciation, where acts of gratitude inspire generosity and goodwill in return. Consider the example of Fred Rogers, whose expressions of gratitude were central to his legacy as a beloved television host. Rogers frequently wrote thank-you notes to fans, collaborators, and friends, cultivating a culture of kindness and appreciation that continues to resonate. His life reminds us that gratitude is not only a personal practice but a bridge that connects us to others.

Gratitude also encourages a mindset of abundance, which is essential for achieving fulfillment. In a culture often driven by comparison and consumerism, gratitude shifts the focus from external markers of success to the richness of the present moment. This perspective aligns with the teachings of Buddhist philosophy, which emphasize the importance of appreciating the present as a source of liberation from desire and attachment. By recognizing the value of what we already have, gratitude fosters a sense of contentment that is independent of external circumstances.

Cultivating gratitude begins with intentionality. Simple practices, such as reflecting on three things one is grateful for each day or writing letters of appreciation to loved ones, can create a ripple effect of positivity. These practices do not require grand gestures or ideal conditions; rather, they thrive in the small, everyday moments that often go unnoticed. For example, taking a moment to appreciate a sunny day, a kind word, or a shared meal can transform routine experiences into sources of joy and connection.

The story of Helen Keller offers a profound illustration of gratitude's transformative power. Despite being deaf and blind from a young age, Keller found immense joy and fulfillment through her education and relationships. Her famous declaration, "Life is either a daring adventure or nothing," reflects her gratitude for the opportunities and connections that shaped her journey. Keller's life demonstrates that gratitude is not contingent on circumstances but on the perspective we choose to embrace.

Gratitude also plays a pivotal role in navigating challenges and adversity. While it may seem counterintuitive, finding reasons to be grateful during difficult times fosters resilience and a sense of agency. Viktor Frankl, who endured the horrors of Nazi concentration camps, described how even small acts of gratitude—such as appreciating a sunset or sharing a piece of bread—helped prisoners maintain their humanity and hope. His insights highlight that gratitude is not about ignoring suffering but about affirming life's value even in its darkest moments.

As individuals reflect on their own lives, they are encouraged to explore the ways in which gratitude can enhance their fulfillment. What aspects of their lives do they appreciate? How can they express this appreciation to others? By integrating gratitude into daily routines and interactions, individuals can create a foundation for joy and resilience that enriches both their inner world and their relationships.

Gratitude is not a static state but a dynamic practice that evolves with experience and perspective. It invites individuals to engage with life fully, recognizing the interconnectedness of all things and the abundance that exists even amidst challenges. In the words of Melody Beattie, "Gratitude makes sense of our past, brings peace for today, and creates a vision for tomorrow." By embracing gratitude, individuals can achieve a deeper sense of fulfillment, finding beauty and meaning in the journey itself.

Embracing Fulfillment as a Lifelong Journey

Fulfillment is not a fixed destination but a dynamic process—a journey that evolves with each stage of life. It transcends the confines of singular achievements, weaving meaning into the fabric of daily existence. This perspective frees individuals from the pressure to chase perfection or reach an ultimate endpoint, instead encouraging them to view fulfillment as a continual exploration of purpose, growth, and connection. Embracing this journey requires openness to change, a willingness to adapt, and a commitment to aligning one's life with deeply held values.

One of the most inspiring examples of fulfillment as a lifelong journey is the story of Nelson Mandela. His life was marked by profound transformations: from young activist to political prisoner, and ultimately to president and global statesman. Each phase of Mandela's life brought new challenges and opportunities to deepen his sense of purpose. During his 27 years of

imprisonment, he cultivated resilience and reflection, using the time to envision a more just
and united South Africa. When he emerged as a
leader, Mandela's commitment to reconciliation
and nation-building reflected his evolving understanding of fulfillment—not as personal triumph, but as service to a greater cause. His life
illustrates that fulfillment is a process shaped by
circumstances and choices, growing richer as
individuals adapt to life's complexities.

Philosophically, the idea of fulfillment as a
journey aligns with the teachings of Buddhism,
which emphasize the impermanence of life and
the importance of being present. In Buddhist
philosophy, fulfillment is not about accumu-
lating accomplishments but about cultivating
mindfulness, compassion, and a sense of interconnectedness. This perspective encourages individuals to find meaning in the present
moment rather than deferring satisfaction to
some imagined future. It also acknowledges
that fulfillment is not linear; it ebbs and flows,
reflecting the ever-changing nature of life.

Modern psychology offers further insights into
fulfillment as an evolving process. Research on

human development, particularly Erik Erikson's stages of psychosocial development, highlights how the quest for meaning and satisfaction shifts across the lifespan. For example, young adulthood often involves seeking identity and purpose, while later stages focus on generativity — contributing to future generations — and reflection on one's legacy. Each phase presents unique opportunities to experience fulfillment, underscoring the importance of embracing life's transitions with curiosity and purpose.

The concept of fulfillment as a journey also resonates in the arts and creative pursuits. Consider the life of Vincent van Gogh, whose path was marked by struggle, reinvention, and relentless exploration. Though van Gogh achieved little recognition during his lifetime, his unwavering commitment to his craft and his search for beauty and meaning in the world brought him a profound sense of purpose. His letters to his brother Theo reveal a deep understanding of fulfillment as a process of discovery, rather than a final outcome. Van Gogh's story reminds us that the pursuit of meaning often involves persistence, experimentation, and the courage to embrace uncertainty.

Practical applications of this perspective begin with reframing how we approach goals and achievements. Rather than viewing success as a series of milestones to be checked off, individuals can focus on aligning their actions with values and aspirations. This shift in mindset fosters a sense of continuity and purpose, even as circumstances change. For instance, a person who values community engagement might volunteer in different capacities throughout their life—mentoring youth, participating in neighborhood projects, or advocating for local causes. These actions, though varied, reflect a consistent thread of purpose that weaves fulfillment into their journey.

Another key aspect of embracing fulfillment as a lifelong journey is resilience—the ability to adapt and find meaning in adversity. Helen Keller's life offers a remarkable example of this principle. Despite the profound challenges of being deaf and blind, Keller found fulfillment through her advocacy for social justice, education, and disability rights. Her work demonstrated that fulfillment is not tied to the absence of obstacles but to the determination to create meaning in their presence. Keller's life inspires individuals to approach setbacks as opportunities for growth, strengthening their sense of purpose along the way.

Fulfillment as a journey also invites individuals to embrace curiosity and continuous learning. Each stage of life offers new perspectives and possibilities, enriching the tapestry of meaning. Mahatma Gandhi once said, "Live as if you were to die tomorrow. Learn as if you were to live forever." This sentiment captures the essence of fulfillment as an evolving process: a balance of urgency and openness, rooted in the understanding that life's richness lies in its unpredictability.

Collaboration and connection further enhance the journey of fulfillment. Relationships play a central role in shaping meaning, offering opportunities to share experiences, exchange ideas, and contribute to others' well-being. Whether through family, friendships, mentorship, or community involvement, these connections provide a sense of belonging and purpose that deepens over time. For example, an educator who invests in their students' growth not only

finds personal fulfillment but also creates a ripple effect of impact that extends far beyond their
own life.

Ultimately, embracing fulfillment as a lifelong
journey requires a willingness to let go of rigid
expectations and embrace the unfolding nature
of life. This perspective encourages individuals
to celebrate progress, however incremental, and
to find joy in the process rather than fixating on
the outcome. It also reminds us that fulfillment
is not a solitary endeavor; it is shaped by the
interplay of personal aspirations, relationships,
and contributions to the broader world.

As readers reflect on their own paths, they are
encouraged to consider how they can embrace
fulfillment as an ongoing process. What values
and aspirations guide their journey? How can
they adapt to life's changes while remaining
true to their purpose? By engaging with these
questions, individuals can cultivate a sense
of fulfillment that grows and evolves, enriching both their own lives and the lives of those
around them.

In the words of Ralph Waldo Emerson, "Life

is a journey, not a destination." This timeless wisdom encapsulates the essence of fulfillment as a dynamic and evolving process. By embracing the journey with openness, resilience, and purpose, individuals can find meaning in every step, creating a life that is as fulfilling as it is impactful.

CONCLUSION: EMBRACING TIMELESS WISDOM IN EVERYDAY LIFE

As we reach the end of this journey through the lessons and legacies of history's greatest minds, one truth emerges clearly: success and fulfillment are deeply personal and infinitely multifaceted. They are not confined to the metrics of wealth or status, nor are they constrained by societal norms or fleeting achievements. Instead, they lie in the alignment of our actions with our values, the resilience we display in the face of adversity, and the connections we cultivate with others. This book has explored the art of building inner strength, fostering meaningful relationships, redefining success, and creating legacies that transcend our own lives. It is now up to you, the reader, to weave these insights into the fabric of your everyday existence.

Throughout history, great thinkers and leaders have demonstrated that fulfillment is not a destination but a dynamic process of becoming. Marcus Aurelius, Viktor Frankl, Helen Keller, and Nelson Mandela each faced unique challenges, yet all found profound meaning in their circumstances. Their lives remind us that fulfillment arises not from the absence of struggle but from the courage to face it with purpose and grace. This resilience, rooted in timeless wisdom, is available to us all. The question is not whether we are capable of finding fulfillment but whether we are willing to embrace the journey with openness and intention.

The Strength Within

The foundation of a fulfilling life lies in building inner strength. As explored in earlier chapters, this strength is not about dominating others or shielding oneself from vulnerability. Rather, it is the quiet fortitude that allows us to persevere, adapt, and grow. Figures like Thomas Edison and Helen Keller exemplified this principle, using setbacks as steppingstones to greater achievements. Their stories teach us that inner strength is cultivated through self-discipline, resilience, and the ability to view challenges as opportunities for growth.

In your own life, consider how you can build this strength. What habits or practices support your mental and emotional well-being? How can you reframe obstacles as invitations to grow? By cultivating inner strength, you create a foundation that enables you to navigate life's complexities with confidence and clarity.

Vision Beyond the Horizon

Fulfillment also requires a visionary mindset — the ability to see beyond immediate circumstances and imagine new possibilities. Leonardo da Vinci, Nikola Tesla, and others like them dared to challenge conventions and dream boldly. Their legacies remind us that vision is not a privilege of the extraordinary but a skill we can all develop. By fostering imagination, embracing curiosity, and pursuing our passions, we expand the horizons of what is possible.

Ask yourself: What is your vision for your life and the world around you? How can you align your actions with this vision to create a future that reflects your deepest values? In answering these questions, you begin to unlock your potential as a creator of change and a source of inspiration.

The Art of Balance

The pursuit of fulfillment often requires navigating the tension between ambition and contentment, action and reflection, striving and being. As explored through the lens of ancient and modern wisdom, balance is not about achieving a perfect equilibrium but about harmonizing the elements of life in ways that reflect your priorities and values. Figures like the Buddha and contemporary mindfulness practitioners remind us of the importance of presence, gratitude, and the ability to let go of what no longer serves us.

Consider how you might cultivate balance in your own life. Are there areas where you are overcommitted or disconnected from what truly matters? How can you create space for reflection, connection, and renewal? By embracing balance as a dynamic process, you create a life that is both purposeful and sustainable.

The Power of Relationships

Fulfillment is never a solitary endeavor; it is shaped by the relationships we nurture and the communities we build. Martin Luther King Jr., Fred Rogers, and countless others understood that meaningful connections are the heart of a life well-lived. They demonstrated the power of trust, empathy, collaboration, and shared purpose in creating change and fostering belonging.

Reflect on the relationships in your own life. How can you deepen trust, show appreciation, or offer support to those around you? What role do you play in your community, and how might you contribute to its growth and well-being? By investing in relationships, you create a network of mutual care and inspiration that enriches both your life and the lives of others.

The Legacy You Leave

As you move through life, consider the legacy you wish to leave. This legacy is not defined solely by grand achievements but by the everyday choices that reflect your values. Whether through acts of kindness, contributions to your field, or the lessons you impart to future generations, your legacy is a testament to the life you have lived.

Figures like Mahatma Gandhi and Jane Addams remind us that legacy is not about personal recognition but about the impact we have on others and the world. What kind of impact do you want to have? How can you begin to shape this legacy today? By aligning your actions with your long-term vision, you ensure that your life's work leaves a meaningful imprint.

The Fulfillment Paradox

Perhaps the most profound lesson of this book is the fulfillment paradox: that true satisfaction is found not in the relentless pursuit of external success but in the alignment of our inner lives with our outer actions. Viktor Frankl's insights into purpose, gratitude, and resilience challenge us to redefine success on our own terms. Fulfillment, as he and others have shown, is not about escaping hardship but about finding meaning within it.

As you consider the insights shared in these pages, ask yourself: What does fulfillment mean to me? How can I align my daily choices with this understanding? By embracing fulfillment as a lifelong journey, you free yourself from the pressure of perfection and open yourself to the joy of becoming.

A Final Invitation

This book is not an endpoint but a beginning — a call to action to live with intention, curiosity, and courage. The wisdom of history's greatest minds is not meant to be admired from a distance but to be applied in the context of your own life. Their stories, lessons, and insights are a reminder that fulfillment is not reserved for the extraordinary but is available to anyone willing to embrace it.

As you close this chapter, consider what steps you can take today to embody the principles of inner strength, vision, balance, connection, and purpose. How can you create a life that reflects your highest aspirations and deepest values? In doing so, you honor the wisdom of those who came before you and contribute to a legacy that will inspire those who follow.

Fulfillment is not a gift to be received but a practice to be lived. It is the courage to face life's uncertainties, the curiosity to explore its possibilities, and the gratitude to appreciate its blessings. By embracing these truths, you create a life that is not only successful by conventional standards but deeply meaningful and profoundly fulfilling.

The journey is yours to take. May it be filled with purpose, resilience, and joy.

ACKNOWLEDGEMENT

This book would not have been possible without the guidance, inspiration, and support of many remarkable individuals.

First and foremost, I extend my deepest gratitude to the thinkers, leaders, and visionaries whose timeless wisdom has shaped the ideas explored within these pages. Their courage, resilience, and insight continue to illuminate the path toward a life of meaning and fulfillment.

To my friends, family, and colleagues, thank you for your unwavering encouragement and belief in this project. Your conversations, perspectives, and feedback have been invaluable, enriching the process at every stage.

A heartfelt thanks to the readers who embark on this journey with me. Your curiosity and commitment to growth are what breathe life into these words. It is my hope that this book serves as a source of inspiration and empowerment in your pursuit of purpose.

Finally, to the unseen forces of creativity and curiosity that make every page a possibility—thank you for reminding us that the search for wisdom is as infinite as it is rewarding. This work is as much yours as it is mine.

ABOUT THE AUTHOR

 Felix Grayson's journey into timeless wisdom began in childhood, captivated by the stories of philosophers, leaders, and visionaries who shaped the way we think and live. Growing up in a home filled with books, he spent countless hours exploring ideas that asked life's biggest questions—a curiosity that would later define his work.

After facing his own modern challenges—balancing ambition, uncertainty, and the search for meaning—Felix discovered that the wisdom of the past offers profound guidance for the present. This realization became the foundation for the *Stoned Philosopher* series: a collection dedicated to translating ancient insights into practical lessons for today's world.

Felix's writing is more than reflection—it's an invitation to dialogue with history's greatest minds. Through each book, he helps readers find clarity, resilience, and purpose in their own lives—one timeless idea at a time.

When not writing, Felix enjoys quiet contemplation, deep conversation, and exploring the endless pursuit of wisdom in everyday moments.

www.ingramcontent.com/pod-product-compliance
Lightning Source LLC
Chambersburg PA
CBHW021234130626
46554CB00004B/1493